Personal tax

(Finance Act 2014)

Tutorial

for assessments from January 2015

Aubrey Penning

Bob Thomas

Published by Osborne Books Limited
Unit 1B Everoak Estate
Bromyard Road, Worcester WR2 5HP
Tel 01905 748071
Email books@osbornebooks.co.uk
Website www.osbornebooks.co.uk

Design by Laura Ingham

Printed by CPI Group (UK) Limited, Croydon, CR0 4YY, on environmentally friendly, acid-free paper from managed forests.

British Library Cataloguing in Publication Data
A catalogue record for this book is available from the British Library

ISBN 978 1909173 491

438081
657.48 (PEN)

Contents

Please note that the seven chapters and subsequent sections of the book each have a self-contained numbering system, rather than the traditional form of pagination which runs through the book.

Acknowledgements

The publisher wishes to thank the following for their help with the reading and production of the book: Jon Moore, Bee Pugh and Cathy Turner. Thanks are also due Laura Ingham for her designs for this series.

The publisher is indebted to the Association of Accounting Technicians for its help and advice to our authors and editors during the preparation of this text.

The publisher would also like to thank HM Revenue & Customs for its help, advice and kind permission to reproduce tax forms obtained from www.hmrc.gov.uk.

Author and Technical Editor

Aubrey Penning has many years experience of teaching accountancy on a variety of courses in Worcester and Gwent. He is a Certified Accountant, and before his move into full-time teaching he worked for the health service, a housing association and a chemical supplier. For many years he was the AAT course coordinator at Worcester College of Technology, specialising in the areas of management accounting and taxation.

Bob Thomas, the Technical Editor of this book, has been involved with the Education and Training activities of the AAT since 1986, including the development and piloting of the skills-based scheme. He is an external verifier, a simulation writer, a moderator and a contributor at workshops, training days, conferences and master classes. Until recently he was a member of the Learning and Development Board and Chairman of the Assessment Panel.

Introduction

what this book covers

This book has been written specifically to cover the 'Personal Tax' Unit which is optional for the AAT Level 4 Diploma in Accounting.

The book contains a clear text with worked examples and case studies, chapter summaries and key terms to help with revision. Each chapter has a wide range of activities, many in the style of the computer-based assessments used by AAT. Note that the pagination of each chapter is self-contained, eg Chapter 1 contains pages 1.0 to 1.23.

Exams, Finance Acts and tax years

This book has been designed to include guidance and exercises based on Tax Year 2014/15 (Finance Act 2014). We understand that the AAT plan to assess this legislation from 1 January 2015 to 31 December 2015. Tutors and students are advised to check this with the AAT and ensure that they sit the correct Computer Based Assessment.

Osborne Workbooks

Osborne Workbooks contain practice material which helps students achieve success in their assessments. *Personal Tax (Finance Act 2014) Workbook* contains a number of paper-based 'fill in' practice exams in the style of the computer-based assessment. Please visit www.osbornebooks.co.uk for further details and access to our online shop.

Tax data

INCOME TAX

Personal allowance

Born after 5 April 1948	£10,000
Born between 6 April 1938 and 5 April 1948	£10,500
Born before 6 April 1938	£10,660

(all subject to restrictions)

Tax rates

	starting rate	basic rate	higher rate	additional rate
General Income	N/A	20%	40%	45%
Savings Income	10%	20%	40%	45%
Dividend Income	N/A	10%	32.5%	37.5%

Tax bands

	£
Starting rate	to 2,880 (Savings Income only)
Basic rate	to 31,865
Higher rate	31,866 – 150,000
Additional rate	over 150,000

Company Car Benefit

% of List Price	g/km
0%	zero
5%*	75 (or less)
11%*	76 – 94
12%*	95
13%*	100
14%*	105

. . . and so on to a maximum of 35%

*add 3% for diesel (to a maximum of 35%)

Company Car Fuel Benefit

Percentage for car (see company car benefit on previous page) x £21,700

Authorised Mileage Rates

Cars and vans	First 10,000 miles in tax year	45p per mile
	Additional mileage	25p per mile
Motor cycles		24p per mile
Bicycles		20p per mile

CAPITAL GAINS TAX

Annual Exempt Amount

£11,000

CGT rate

Gains   18% or 28%

1 Introduction to income tax

this chapter covers...

In this chapter we provide a brief review of the UK tax system and an introduction to the income tax computation.

We will then examine how income is divided up into categories for income tax purposes, and what the main rules (the 'basis of assessment') are for each of these categories.

Next we will learn how to calculate income tax, including using the personal allowance and the tax rates for general income. This is illustrated with examples and case study.

We will then see how a tax return is structured, and what the submission dates are. Also examined are the main forms of exempt income that should be omitted from a tax return and do not incur tax liabilities.

The dates of payment of income tax are outlined next, along with important dates in the tax calendar.

Finally we will examine the responsibilities of both the taxpayer and the tax practitioner, including those relating to confidentiality and record keeping.

A REVIEW OF THE UK TAX SYSTEM

When the word 'tax' is mentioned most people probably think of income tax (if they can bear to think of tax at all). Income tax is only one of the forms of taxation that is used to collect money for use by the UK government, but it does impact on a large proportion of the UK population.

In the first part of this book we will be examining how income tax works, and how we can calculate how much income tax individuals should pay. In the second part of the book we will be looking at how capital gains tax can affect individuals if they dispose of certain personal assets. We will also learn how to complete the tax returns for these taxes.

In the Unit 'Personal Tax' we deal only with income tax and capital gains tax, and therefore we will be ignoring other taxes such as value added tax, corporation tax, and inheritance tax. National insurance contributions are also outside the scope of this unit.

We will now look at some of the background to the way that the tax system works, before going on to see how the numerical tax calculations work.

HM Revenue & Customs

Income tax and capital gains tax are both administered by the government department, formed by the amalgamation of the Inland Revenue and HM Customs & Excise. HM Revenue & Customs contains the following three parts:

- **taxpayer service offices** are the main offices that the taxpayer deals with, and handle much of the basic income tax assessment and collection functions
- **taxpayer district offices** deal with more complex income tax issues
- **tax enquiry centres** deal with enquiries and provide forms and leaflets to taxpayers

These three functions are located in offices throughout the UK. In smaller centres some functions may be combined into one office, while in larger towns and cities they may be located separately.

the law governing tax

The authority to impose taxes comes from two sources. The first is legislation passed by parliament, known as 'statute law'. You may have heard of the 'Finance Acts'. These are generally published each year and give details of any changes to taxes. These changes will have been proposed by the Chancellor of the Exchequer (usually in 'the budget') and passed by Parliament. In this book we will be using information from the Finance Act 2014, which relates to the tax year 2014/15. We will see exactly what is meant by tax years later in this chapter.

There are also other statute laws that were designed to create frameworks for the way that certain taxes work that continue to be relevant.

The second source of tax law is called 'case law', and arises from decisions taken in court cases. Taxation can be very complicated, and sometimes disagreements between HM Revenue & Customs and taxpayers result in court cases. The final outcome of such cases can then become 'case law' and influence future interpretation of statute law.

Although there is a substantial amount of both statute law and case law that governs the UK tax system, this book will try to keep references to specific law to a minimum. While it will be important to know the rules that apply to certain situations, you will not be required to quote from the legislation.

information available from HM Revenue & Customs

In addition to the tax law outlined above, there are interpretations and explanations of various issues that are published by HM Revenue & Customs. The main ones are as follows:

- extra-statutory concessions are issued by HM Revenue & Customs when they agree to impose a less strict interpretation of the law than would otherwise apply in particular circumstances
- HM Revenue & Customs statements of practice are public announcements of how the HMRC interpret specific rules
- Guides and Help Sheets are issued to help taxpayers complete the necessary return forms and calculate their tax

A large array of publications and forms can be downloaded from the HM Revenue & Customs website at www.hmrc.gov.uk. It also provides data on rates and allowances for a range of tax years. You will find it useful to have a look at what is available on this site when you have an opportunity. It will also mean that you can obtain copies of tax returns to practice on when you reach that part of your personal tax studies. The HM Revenue & Customs website can also be accessed via a link from the Osborne Books Limited website at www.osbornebooks.co.uk

AN INTRODUCTION TO INCOME TAX COMPUTATION

An outline of an income tax computation is as follows:

	£
Income – both earnings and income from savings	X
Less: Personal allowance	(X)
Taxable Income	X
Tax payable on taxable income	X

A very simple income tax computation could be as follows:

	£
Income from earnings	12,000
Less: Personal Allowance	10,000
Taxable income	2,000
Tax payable at 20%	400

Later in this chapter we will deal with income tax computations in more detail, but first we will consider some of the issues that might arise in computing income tax.

HOW INCOME IS DIVIDED UP FOR TAX PURPOSES

The income that an individual generates is divided into categories, depending on what sort of income it is and where it comes from. The categories are simply named after the type of income that they include. This is done so that:

■ the correct rules on how to work out the income are used (since these vary with the categories), and

■ the correct rates of tax are used (since they can also depend on the type of income)

the main categories of income

'Property Income'	Rental income from land and property.
'Trading Income'	Profits of trades and professions (the self-employed and those in partnership).
'Savings & Investment Income'	UK Interest and UK Dividends.
'Employment, pension and Social Security Income'	Income from employment etc. Income tax is deducted from employment income under the system known as Pay-As-You-Earn (PAYE).

This list and descriptions have been simplified to include only the types of income that you need to know about. It does not include, for example, the categories that relate to overseas income.

tax years

For income tax purposes time is divided into 'tax years' (sometimes called 'fiscal years'). Individuals' income and income tax is worked out separately for each tax year. The tax year runs from 6 April in one calendar year to 5 April in the next calendar year. The tax year running from 6/4/14 to 5/4/15 would be described as the tax year 2014/15.

basis of assessment

As mentioned earlier, the income under each category will have different rules that determine how the income is worked out for tax purposes. The most important of these rules is known as the 'basis of assessment', and this simply considers whether the income assessable is the actual income *receivable* (the accruals basis) or the income *received* in the tax year itself. Later in the book we will look in more detail at the rules that govern each type of income. Here is a list of the main assessment rules for each category of income, with some comments about coverage in this book.

Property Income	**Rental income (after deducting allowable expenses), for the tax year, calculated on an *accruals* basis.**
	We will look in more detail at rental income in Chapter 2.
Trading Income	**Profits on an *accruals* basis (after deducting allowable expenses) for the accounting year that ends in the tax year.**
	In this unit we only need to be aware that profits of the self-employed are included in the income tax calculations of individuals. The calculation of the profit for trading income is dealt with in the Business Tax unit.
Savings and Investment Income	**Gross interest *received* in the tax year.** **Amounts of dividends *received* in the tax year, plus the related tax credits.**
	We will look in more detail at interest received and dividends in Chapter 3.

Employment, Pension and Social Security Income	Amounts *received* in the tax year from employment etc, plus the value of any benefits, less any allowable deductions.

We will examine employment income in detail in Chapter 4.

HOW INCOME TAX IS CALCULATED

As already stated, income tax is usually worked out by using an 'income tax computation' for a specific tax year. This is a calculation that simply brings together the amounts of income from the various categories that apply to the individual and shows the workings for the tax that is payable. It is important that you are able to calculate an individual's income tax, so you will need to learn the basic computation structure and practice plenty of examples. The computation can be understood quite easily if we think of it as divided into three main parts.

1   The first part collects together and adds up the income from the different categories that are relevant. It is also a good idea to note in the computation any tax that has already been paid or deducted from each of these income sources, so that we can account for it later on. In complicated situations it will be necessary to calculate the income under each of the categories separately before the main computation is attempted.

2   The second part of the computation is where personal allowances are deducted from the total income from the first section. Every individual (apart from those with very high income) has a personal allowance for each tax year. This represents the tax-free portion of their income for that year. The final figure that results from this section is known as the 'taxable income'.

3   The third part of the computation is where the taxable income from the previous part is used to calculate the amount of income tax. This is carried out using 'tax bands' and the percentage income tax rates that apply to each band. The total tax from this calculation is then compared with the amount already paid to arrive at the amount still owing to HM Revenue & Customs (or to the taxpayer).

Throughout this book we will use the allowances and tax bands relating to 2014/15. Whatever tax year is used, the principles and process are the same.

Full details of allowances and tax bands can be found at the beginning of this book. The majority of this data will also be provided in your examination.

personal allowance

The basic personal allowance is £10,000 for 2014/15. This is the amount that an individual's income can amount to in the tax year before they start paying income tax. It is always deducted from total income in the computation before the tax is calculated. Individuals with very high income (over £100,000) will have their personal allowances reduced or eliminated. We will see how this works in detail in Chapter 5. There are different allowances for those born before 5 April 1948 (aged 66 and over at the start of the tax year), and we will also learn about these allowances in Chapter 5.

tax bands

The tax bands apply to an individual's taxable income – their total income for the year after the personal allowance has been deducted. The tax is calculated by multiplying the percentage shown by the income that falls into each band. This is done by starting with the lowest band and working up as far as necessary. The 2014/15 rates and bands are shown here:

Tax Bands for tax year 2014/15 – General Income		
Rate	**Taxable Income**	
20%	(Basic rate)	up to £31,865
40%	(Higher rate)	£31,866 to £150,000
45%	(Additional rate)	over £150,000

Note that there are other tax bands and rates for savings and investment income (interest and dividends) – we will look at these later in the book.

This diagram shows how it works:

So, for example, if an individual had taxable general income (after deducting their personal allowance) of £20,000 in 2014/15, the tax would be:

£ 20,000 x 20%   =   £4,000.00

Remember that 'income' can include not only earnings from a job but also other forms of income.

The total income tax relating to a tax year is often referred to as the 'Income Tax Liability'. We will now use a Case Study to show the full process for a simple tax computation.

Case Study

SHELLEY BEECH:
BASIC INCOME TAX COMPUTATION

Shelley Beech works as an employee for a recruitment company. In 2014/15 she received £35,000 in income from this job, before her employer deducted £5,000 in income tax through PAYE.
She also received rent from the house that she had originally been left by her grandfather. The taxable amount of rent for 2014/15 has already been worked out as £10,500, but she hasn't paid any income tax on this yet.
Shelley is entitled to the basic personal allowance of £10,000 for the tax year.

required
Using an income tax computation, calculate the total income tax that Shelley is liable to pay for the tax year 2014/15, and how much of this amount has not yet been paid.

solution
Following the format discussed earlier, we can produce an income tax computation as follows:

Shelley Beech – Income Tax Computation for 2014/15

	£	£
		Tax Paid
Employment Income	35,000	5,000
Property Income (rent)	10,500	–
Total Income	45,500	5,000
Less Personal Allowance	10,000	
Taxable Income	35,500	

Income Tax Calculation

£31,865 x 20%		6,373.00
£3,635 x 40%		1,454.00
£35,500	Total Income tax	7,827.00
	Less already paid	5,000.00
	Income tax to pay	2,827.00

To understand the above computation, you should note the following:

• The tax deducted at source is noted in the column on the right. The total of this column is then used in the final calculation to work out how much of the total tax is still unpaid.

• In this Case Study the taxable income of £35,500 is more than the £31,865 that forms the upper point of the 20% tax band. This means that the entire 20% band is used, as well as some of the 40% band. The income is not high enough to reach the 45% tax band.

• The amount of taxable income to be taxed at 40% is calculated by deducting the amounts charged at 20% from the taxable income (£35,500 – £31,865 = £3,635).

HOW AN INDIVIDUAL'S TAX RETURN WORKS

The Tax Return is a document used by HM Revenue & Customs to collect information about an individual's income and capital gains. It is not sent out to every taxpayer – those who have uncomplicated income may never receive the form. This is because the mechanisms of Pay-As-You-Earn and other deductions of tax at source can often deal with these situations.

The types of situation that we are going to be studying are ones where the tax position is a little more complicated. These individuals may have income from several sources (perhaps including self-employed income, and/or income from rent), and may involve paying tax at the higher rate and additional rate. Because HM Revenue & Customs will need to know all these individual's income details, a tax return must be completed. The current tax return operates under the 'self-assessment' system, whereby an individual declares his/her income and gains, and has the option of calculating his/her own tax. The tax return form therefore has the purposes of both itemising the income, and recording the amount of tax due.

structure of the tax return

Because different individuals have different circumstances, the standard tax return is divided into two parts.

The first part is used by everyone who needs a standard tax return, and is therefore common to all these returns. It requests general information, as well as details of:

- income from UK savings and investments
- income from pensions and social security benefits
- reliefs claimed for various expenditure
- specific allowances claimed
- the income tax due

The second part of the tax return consists of a series of supplementary pages that are only used by relevant taxpayers. The main supplementary pages are for:

- employment income
- self-employment income
- partnership income
- income from UK property
- capital gains (profits made on selling assets)

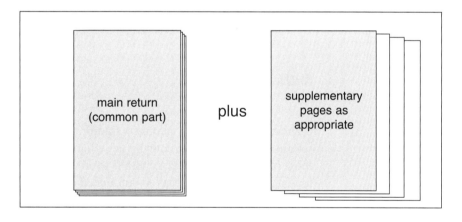

An online version of the tax return can also be completed and submitted electronically as an alternative to the traditional paper-based version. Whether the tax return is submitted online or in paper-based form makes a difference to when it must be submitted by.

timing of the tax return

Around the end of the tax year (April 2015 for the tax year 2014/15) the following will happen. Relevant taxpayers will either be sent a paper tax return to complete, or a reminder that they need to submit an online return (if that's the way they have submitted previously).

The latest submission dates are as follows:

- paper-based returns need to be submitted by 31 October following the end of the tax year. Provided they are correctly completed HMRC will then calculate the tax if the taxpayer (or agent) hasn't already done so. For the tax year 2014/15 the final date for paper returns is therefore 31 October 2015

- online submissions need to be made by 31 January following the end of the tax year. This provides an incentive to submit online since taxpayers have a deadline 3 months later than for the paper-based forms. Another advantage of submitting online is that the computer software automatically calculates the tax as the data is inserted. The online deadline for the tax year 2014/15 is therefore 31 January 2016

An example of a tax return is reproduced in the appendix to this book. The return forms are also available from the HM Revenue & Customs website. As we progress through this book we will examine in detail how various parts of the return should be completed.

SHORT TAX RETURN

Some of the individuals who have traditionally received self-assessment tax returns as just described, actually have fairly straightforward tax affairs. For these individuals a short tax return is available. This return is only four pages long and is designed so that an automated data capture system can be used.

The short return is only sent to those selected individuals who may have modest income from property or savings, in addition to income from:

- employment (other than company directors)
- self-employment (with turnover less than £79,000 p.a. [2013/14 figure])
- pensions

EXEMPT INCOME

Exempt income is outside the scope of income tax. Exempt income will not have had tax deducted from it at source, and it should not appear anywhere in the income tax computation. You should make sure that you are familiar with the following abbreviated list of exempt income, since it is possible that items from it could be included in an examination task to test your ability to select the right income to include in a tax computation.

- Prizes are generally exempt from income tax. These include:
  - Premium Bond prizes
  - Lottery prizes (of any amount)
  - betting winnings (unless a professional gambler)

- Income from ISAs and New ISAs (NISAs) are specifically exempt. This form of investment has been designed by the government to encourage saving and investment by exempting the income from tax.

- Damages arising from personal injury or death.

- Educational grants.

We will look at savings and investment income in detail in Chapter 3.

We will now use a further Case Study to see how some of the issues covered in this chapter can be dealt with all together.

Case Study

MARK DOWNE: INCOME FROM VARIOUS SOURCES

Mark Downe is a self-employed market trader. His profits (adjusted for income tax purposes) for the last two accounting periods were as follows:

Year ended 30/6/14	£30,000
Year ended 30/6/15	£28,000

He also has income from a house that he rents out to students. The following profits from this have been calculated on an accruals basis and adjusted for tax purposes.

6/4/2013 - 5/4/2014	£10,500
6/4/2014 - 5/4/2015	£13,000
6/4/2015 - 5/4/2016	£14,000

Mark won £12,000 on the National Lottery on 15 June 2014.

He was also employed as a part time barman from 1/7/2014 to 30/6/2015. He was paid on the last day of each month that he worked, and his monthly gross pay during this time was £500. He paid £900 under PAYE in 2014/15, and £300 in 2015/16.

Mark invested in a NISA in 2014/15. This generated interest of £120 in that tax year.

required

1 Using an income tax computation, calculate Mark's income tax liability for 2014/15.

2 Specify which supplementary pages he will need to complete in his tax return for 2014/15, and state the latest date that the paper-based form should be returned to HM Revenue & Customs.

solution

This is more complicated than the last Case Study, since we are given a lot more information about the taxpayer's income, some of which relates to a different tax year, and some of which is not taxable at all.

The income that should go into the tax computation for 2014/15 comprises:

- the profits from his self-employment for the accounting period ending in the tax year 2014/15, ie the profits for the year to 30/6/14: £30,000

- the rental income for the period 6/4/2014 to 5/4/2015: £13,000

- the part time bar work earnings received between 1/7/2014 and 5/4/2015, ie 9 months x £500 = £4,500

The lottery winnings and the interest from the NISA are both exempt.

We can now complete the income tax computation as follows:

1   **Mark Downe – Income Tax Computation for 2014/15**

	£	£
		Tax Paid
Trading Income	30,000	-
Employment Income	4,500	900
Property Income (rent)	13,000	-
Total Income	47,500	900
Less Personal Allowance	10,000	
Taxable Income	37,500	

Income Tax Calculation

£31,865 x 20%		6,373.00
£5,635 x 40%		2,254.00
£37,500	Income Tax Liability	8,627.00
	Less already paid	900.00
	Income tax to pay	7,727.00

2 Mark will need the supplementary tax return pages for employment, self-employment, and rental income, in addition to the common pages. He must complete the form for 2014/15 and return it to HM Revenue & Customs by 31 October 2015 at the latest.

WHEN TO PAY INCOME TAX

Some income tax is paid when the income that it relates to is generated. For example under the Pay-As-You-Earn system income tax is deducted from employment income by the employer, and paid over to HM Revenue & Customs on the taxpayer's behalf. In a similar way many forms of savings income have tax deducted at source by (for example) a bank or building society.

For other types of income there is no system set up to automatically deduct income tax. Rental income and income from self-employment are two examples of income where this is usually the case.

As we saw in the previous Case Studies, an income tax computation can be used to calculate both the total income tax liability and the part of this amount that has yet to be paid. It is this outstanding balance of income tax that will need to be paid to HM Revenue & Customs according to the following rules.

■ The **final** date for payment of the income tax that relates to a tax year is the 31 January **following the end of that tax year.**

■ For some taxpayers there may also be payments on account that must be made before the final date. These are due as follows:

- The first payment on account is due on the **31 January within the tax year.**

- The second payment on account is due on the **31 July following the end of the tax year.**

So for the tax year 2014/15 the payment dates would be:

31 January 2015 for the first payment on account,

31 July 2015 for the second payment on account, and

31 January 2016 for the final payment.

For the tax year 2015/16 the payment dates would be:

31 January 2016 for the first payment on account,

31 July 2016 for the second payment on account, and

31 January 2017 for the final payment.

Notice that when payments on account are required, two payments will be due on each 31 January. For example, on 31 January 2016 there would be due both:

■ the final payment for the tax year 2014/15, and

■ the first payment on account for the tax year 2015/16

Later in the book we will see how the payments on account are calculated, and which taxpayers need to make these early payments.

We saw earlier that the 31 January following the tax year was also the final date for submitting an online tax return, so we can build up the following calendar of key dates for the tax years that we are concerned with.

Sample Income Tax Timetable		
	Re Tax Year 2014/15	**Re Tax Year 2015/16**
31 Jan 15	First payment on account of income tax	
April 2015	2014/15 Tax Return Issued (or online reminder)	
31 July 15	Second payment on account of income tax	

31 Oct 15	Return to be filed if paper-based.	
31 Jan 16	Return to be filed if online submission used.	
	Payment of final amount of income tax for 2014/15	First payment on account of income tax for 2015/16
April 2016		Tax Return Issued (or online reminder)
31 July 16		Second payment on account of income tax
31 Oct 16		Return to be filed if paper-based.
31 Jan 17		Return to be filed if online submission used.
		Payment of final amount of income tax

RESPONSIBILITIES OF THE TAXPAYER

The taxpayer should always be open and honest in any dealings with HMRC. **It is the taxpayer's responsibility to inform HMRC if they have any taxable income or gains on which tax has not been paid.**

If the taxpayer normally receives a tax return or submits one online, then all taxable income and gains should be notified on the return. If the taxpayer does not normally need to complete a return, then it is the taxpayer's responsibility to inform HMRC of any source of income that they are not aware of and they will then need to complete a tax return.

For those who do not normally complete a tax return, income that has tax deducted at source (for example employment income taxed under PAYE or interest where tax has been deducted) does not need to be notified. However where no tax has been deducted from income from some source(s) then it is the taxpayer's responsibility to notify HMRC. This could relate, for example, to interest received gross.

There is a general time limit for notifying HMRC about sources of taxable income (called 'notification of chargeability') which is 5 October following the end of the tax year. There are penalties for not complying with this.

Penalties are discussed in Chapter 5.

It is also the taxpayer's responsibility to keep records for the appropriate length of time. If the taxpayer is using a tax practitioner, then they may hold the records for the taxpayer. The details of the time periods are outlined in the next section, and there are summaries of the type of records that are needed for various sources of income in the relevant chapters of this book. There can be a penalty for not keeping the required records of up to £3,000 for each tax year.

tax avoidance and tax evasion

It is important to distinguish between the legal practice of tax avoidance, and tax evasion, which is illegal. Tax avoidance involves using legitimate tax rules and allowances to minimise the amount of tax that is due. This could include investing in NISAs so that any interest received is tax free.

Tax evasion involves using illegal methods to escape paying the correct amount of tax. Examples would include entering false information in a tax return or failing to notify HMRC about a taxable source of income on which tax has not been paid. Those who carry out tax evasion risk criminal prosecution.

THE DUTIES AND RESPONSIBILITIES OF A TAX PRACTITIONER

A **tax practitioner** is someone who helps clients on a professional basis with their tax affairs. The practitioner has responsibilities both:

- to the client, and
- to HM Revenue & Customs

The greatest duty of care is to the client, but the tax practitioner must always act within the law.

The AAT has published a revised 'Code of Professional Ethics' that deals with these and other issues. These apply to AAT students and members. The document can be downloaded from the website at www.aat.org.uk

With regard to **confidentiality** in general, the guidelines state that confidentiality should always be observed unless either:

- authority has been given to disclose the information (by the client), or
- there is a legal or professional right or duty to disclose information

The Code also says that:

> *'Information about a past, present, or prospective client's or employer's affairs, or the affairs of clients of employers, acquired in a work context is likely to be confidential if it is not a matter of public knowledge.'*

The rules of confidentiality apply in a social environment as well as a business one, and care should be taken to not inadvertently disclose confidential information. The need to comply also extends after a business relationship has ended – for example if there was a change of employment.

One important **exception to the normal rules of confidentiality** is where **'money laundering'** is known or suspected. 'Money laundering' includes any process of concealing or disguising the proceeds of any criminal offence, including tax evasion.

Where a practitioner has knowledge or suspicion that his client is money laundering, then he has a duty to inform the relevant person or authority. For those in a group practice this would be the Money Laundering Reporting Officer (MLRO), and for sole practitioner the Serious Organised Crime Agency (SOCA).

It is an offence to warn the client that a report of this type is going to be made about him. Money laundering therefore is not a situation where authority would be sought from the client to disclose information!

The Code states the following regarding taxation services:

> *'A member providing professional tax services has a duty to put forward the best position in favour of a client or an employer. However the service must be carried out with professional competence, must not in any way impair integrity or objectivity, and must be consistent with the law.'*

The Code also states that:

> *'A member shall only undertake taxation work on the basis of full disclosure by the client or employer. The member, in dealing with the tax authorities, must act in good faith and exercise care in relation to facts and information presented on behalf of the client or employer. It will normally be assumed that facts and information on which business tax computations are based were provided by the client or employer as the taxpayer, and the latter bears ultimate resopnsibility for the accuracy of the facts, information and tax computations. The member shall avoid assuming responsibility for the accuracy of facts, etc. outside his or her knowledge.*
>
> *'When a member learns of a material error or omission in a tax return of a prior year, or of a failure to file a required tax return, the member has a responsibility to advise promptly the client or employer of the error or omission and recommend that disclosure be made to HMRC. If the client*

or employer, after having had a reasonable time to reflect, does not correct the error, the member shall inform the client or employer in writing that it is not possible for the member to act for them in connection with that return or other related information submitted to the authorities.'

Dealing with professional ethics can be a difficult and complex area, and we have only outlined some main points. If you find yourself in a position where you are uncertain how you should proceed because of an ethical problem then you should first approach your supervisor or manager. If you are still unable to resolve the problem then further professional or legal advice may need to be obtained.

keeping records

It will also be important to know what records will need to be kept regarding the client's income and tax affairs, and to ensure that such records are kept secure. The records must be sufficient to substantiate the information provided to HM Revenue & Customs. This would include documentation such as invoices, receipts, and working papers. These records must be kept as follows:

- in general records must be retained for approximately 1 year plus 10 months from the end of the tax year to which they relate. For example documents relating to 2014/15 must be retained until 31 January 2017. This is one year after the latest filing date for that year's online tax return

- for those in business or clients who let property, the time is extended to approximately 5 years plus 10 months from the end of the tax year. If there is a formal HM Revenue & Customs enquiry into a taxpayer's affairs then the records need to be kept at least until the end of the enquiry

compliance checks

HMRC can carry out 'compliance checks' relating to a range of taxes including Income Tax and Capital Gains Tax to ensure that the correct amount of tax is paid and that proper records are kept. HMRC have powers to:

- visit businesses to inspect premises, assets and records
- ask taxpayers and third parties (for example tax practitioners) for more information and documents

In most situations at least seven days prior notice would be given of a visit. HMRC are required by law to 'act reasonably' with regard to compliance checks.

Chapter Summary

■   Income tax in the UK is administered by HM Revenue & Customs. It is responsible for publishing documents and forms to gather information about how much tax is owed, and collecting the tax on behalf of the government. It is governed by statute law and case law.

■   Income is divided into categories so that appropriate rules can be applied to calculate the amount of each different form of income.

■   Income tax is calculated separately for each tax year, that runs from 6 April to the following 5 April. An income tax computation is used to calculate the tax by totalling the income from various sources, and subtracting allowances. The income tax is then calculated by reference to the tax bands and rates that relate to the tax year.

■   Tax returns are used to collect information about individuals' income and tax each year. They consist of a common section plus supplementary pages that depend on the taxpayer's circumstances.

■   Some specific forms of income are exempt from income tax and should not be included on the tax return.

■   Income tax that has not been paid by deduction must be paid to HM Revenue & Customs by the 31 January following the end of the tax year. For some taxpayers there is also a requirement to make payments on account before this date.

■   Tax practitioners have responsibilities to their clients (including confidentiality) and to HM Revenue & Customs. They must also ensure that all necessary records are kept for the required period of time.

Key Terms

statute law — legislation that is passed by parliament – an example of statute law relating to taxation is the Finance Act 2014

case law — the result of decisions taken in court cases that have an impact on the interpretation of law

tax year — each tax year runs from 6 April to the following 5 April – tax years are also known as fiscal years

basis of assessment — the rule that decides what income from a particular source is taxable for a tax year – eg the basis of assessment for trading income is normally the adjusted profits of the accounting period that ends in the tax year

income tax computation — the format used to calculate income tax – it collates income from various sources, subtracts personal allowances, and calculates tax on the resultant taxable income

personal allowance — the amount that an individual's income can amount to before tax is charged – in 2014/15 the basic personal allowance is £10,000

taxable income — an individual's income after subtracting the personal allowance – it is the amount that is used to calculate the tax liability

tax bands — income tax is charged at various percentage rates according to the type of income and the tax bands – for example the 20% tax band for general income in 2014/15 relates to taxable income up to £31,865

tax return — the self-assessment tax return is issued annually to certain taxpayers – it is divided into a common section, plus supplementary pages that relate to the taxpayer's circumstances

exempt income — income that is not chargeable to income tax and should therefore not be shown on the tax return or in the tax computation

Activities

> *Note: in these Student Activities the words 'year end' are abbreviated to 'y/e' and dates are quoted in the format '30/9/09'.*

1.1   The following are statements made by a trainee in the tax department:

(a)   One of the reasons that income is divided into categories is so that the correct rules can be applied to each type of income.

(b)   When examining the tax rules for 2014/15, the only law that is relevant is the Finance Act 2014.

(c)   Every individual will receive a tax return each year that they must complete.

(d)   All income must be declared on the tax return and used in the income tax computation.

(e)   Taxable income is the name given to total income (apart from exempt income) after basic personal allowances have been subtracted.

(f)   An individual with only general taxable income of £1,500 in 2014/15 would pay income tax of £300.

(g)   It is the job of a tax practitioner to ensure that his client pays the least amount of tax. This may involve bending the rules, or omitting certain items from a tax computation.

(h)   Most self-employed people pay tax under PAYE and so don't have to worry about completing tax returns.

(i)   A lottery win of over £250,000 is taxable.

Required:

Select those statements that are true.

1.2 Mary has the following income:

Salary of £1,000 per month from her employment throughout 2014 and 2015, plus bonuses paid as follows:

>   £300 paid in May 2014 re y/e 31/12/13
>
>   £500 paid in May 2015 re y/e 31/12/14

Mary had £460 deducted under PAYE during 2014/15.

Part time self-employed business – profits as follows:

>   y/e 30/9/14   £2,800
>
>   y/e 30/9/15   £2,750

She also rents out a property that she owns. She received £4,500 in rent for the period 6/4/14 - 5/4/15 after deducting allowable costs.

Required:

Using an Income Tax Computation for 2014/15, calculate Mary's total income tax liability, and how much of it has not been paid.

1.3 The following is a list of the sources of Sue's income for the tax year.

(a)   Dividends from shares in UK companies

(b)   Income from employment as a Sales Manager

(c)   Interest from a NISA

(d)   Interest from a bank deposit account

(e)   Winnings from a bet on the Grand National

(f)   Rent received from a property let to students

Required:

For each income source either state which category it should be included under, or state that it is exempt from income tax.

1.4 John has the following income:

- wages from employment £660 per month

- rental income from a house left to him by his Grandmother, due on the last day of each month. The £250 per month for the months of April 2014 - February 2015 were paid on time. The £250 for March 2015 was paid on 30/4/15 along with the April rent

- there were no allowable expenses to be deducted from this rental income

- interest Earned on NISA with B&B Building Society, £230

John paid nothing during 2014/15 under PAYE.

Required:

Using an Income Tax Computation for the tax year, calculate John's total income tax liability, and how much of it has not been paid.

1.5   Megan has the following income:

Salary of £2,800 per month from her employment throughout 2014 and 2015, plus bonuses paid as follows:

£800 paid in September 2014 re y/e 31/3/14

£500 paid in September 2015 re y/e 31/3/15

Megan had £4,880 deducted under PAYE during 2014/15.

Income from writing articles for technical magazines, categorised as trading income, as follows:

year ended 31/12/14	£14,700
year ended 31/12/15	£16,350

Required:

Using an Income Tax Computation for the tax year, calculate Megan's total income tax liability, and how much of it has not been paid.

1.6   **Required:**

State whether each of the following statements is true or false.

(a)   Every individual's tax records need to be kept until approximately 5 years and 10 months after the end of the tax year.

(b)   It is the taxpayer's responsibility to inform HMRC of any untaxed taxable income, even if they haven't been sent a tax return.

(c)   Accountants must follow the rules of confidentiality in all situations.

(d)   Confidentiality rules do not apply after the end of a business relationship, or in a social environment.

(e)   Accountants are allowed to break the rules of confidentiality when money laundering is suspected.

(f)   When an accountant is advising a client the greatest duty of care is to HMRC.

2 Income from property

this chapter covers...

In this chapter we will examine how income from rented UK property is taxed. We will start by examining what exactly is covered by the rules that we need to learn, and then see how the accruals basis is applied to this type of income.

We will look in detail at the expenditure that is 'allowable' – that which can reduce the taxable amount. We will contrast this with disallowable expenditure, and see how a calculation of taxable profit is carried out for both individual and multiple properties.

Next we will examine how relief can be claimed under the 'rent a room' scheme when part of the home that a taxpayer occupies is rented out on a furnished basis (for example to a lodger). We will see that this relief can also apply to operations that also supply services, like guest houses.

Holiday lets are examined in the following section. This is followed by a summary of how rental losses can be offset.

Finally we will illustrate completion of the tax return supplementary pages for UK property, and summarise the records that should be kept by a landlord or his agent.

HOW PROPERTY INCOME IS TAXED

what does Property Income cover?

Property income can include:

- income from renting out land
- income from renting out unfurnished property
- income from renting out furnished property

The term 'property' is used to mean buildings, either residential (flats, houses, etc) or commercial (offices etc). Furnished holiday letting income is also taxed as property income. The general rules that we will study in this chapter apply to holiday lettings as well as other property rentals.

You may be asked to calculate the amount assessable relating to one or more properties that are rented out by a client. The client is usually the owner of the properties, but it would be possible for him to have rented them from another landlord. The landlord may have bought the property specifically to rent out. This is known as 'buy to let'.

There are special rules that can apply when someone is renting out part of the house that they live in. We will examine this 'rent a room' scheme later in the chapter.

accruals basis of calculation

You may remember from the last chapter that a 'basis of assessment' sets out the way that income is calculated and linked to tax years. The basis of assessment for property income is **profits** from land and property **for the tax year**, calculated on an **accruals** basis.

This means the income should therefore relate to the tax year in which it will be assessed. For example, for the tax year 2014/15 this would be the period 6/4/14 to 5/4/15.

You need to be clear about the distinction between:

- the accruals basis that we use here. (This is the same basis that applies to statements of profit or loss (income statements) under normal financial accounting rules), and
- the receipts (or cash) basis that does not apply to this category, but applies (for example) to salaries and wages

Because property income is calculated on an accruals basis, the assessable rental income is that which **relates to the tax year**. So, for example, (assuming an ongoing tenancy):

- if a tenant had paid more than one year's worth of rent during the tax year, only the amount that related to the tax year would be assessable in the tax year

- if a tenant had fallen behind with his rental payments, the amount that related to the tax year would still be assessable in that year, even though it hadn't all been received. This is provided the tenant was able to pay it eventually

One issue to be careful about is where an unpaid amount of rent is considered 'irrecoverable'. In these circumstances the irrecoverable amount can be deducted from the rental income. This is exactly the same logic that occurs in financial accounting, when 'irrecoverable debts' are written off.

Case Study

MINNIE STREET: ASSESSABLE RENT

Minnie Street rents out two unfurnished properties to tenants. Each has a monthly rental of £500, payable in advance on the 6th day of each month.

From January 2014 onwards, the following rents were paid:

The tenant of property one paid the rent on time every month during 2014. On 6 January 2015 he paid six months rent in advance since he was going on a long holiday.

The tenant of property two also paid the rent on time every month during 2014. During 2015 he failed to pay any rent. He left the property on 5 March, without leaving a forwarding address or paying the rent that he owed. Minnie has been unable to locate him since then. Property two was re-let to another tenant in May 2015.

required

Calculate the assessable amount under property income for Minnie Street for the tax year 2014/15.

solution

The assessable amount for **property one** is 12 x £500 = £6,000. The extra rent paid in advance by the tenant that relates to the period after 6/4/2015 will be assessable in the following tax year.

The assessable amount for **property two** is calculated as:

Relating to the period of occupation
    6/4/2014 - 5/3/2015   11 x £500   = £5,500

Less irrecoverable amounts (relating to
rent due in January and February but not paid)   2 x £500   = £1,000

                                                                    £4,500

Since property two is not rented out in the period 6/3/2015 to 5/4/2015 there is no assessable amount for this month.

The total amount assessable as property income for Minnie Street for 2014/15 is therefore £6,000 + £4,500 = £10,500.

EXPENDITURE THAT IS ALLOWABLE

'Allowable' expenditure is expenditure that can be deducted from the rental income to arrive at the assessable property income.

Note that some expenditure that is quite proper from an accounting point of view may not be 'allowable' for taxation purposes. This does not mean that the accounts produced are necessarily wrong, but we will need to make adjustments before they are suitable for our tax work.

The general rule for expenditure to be allowable in a property income calculation is that it must be:

■ revenue rather than capital in nature, and

■ 'wholly and exclusively' for the purpose of lettings

Allowable expenditure may include:

■ business rates, water rates and council tax – this would apply where the landlord has paid these items, effectively on behalf of the tenant – the rent would have been set at such a level to allow for the fact that the landlord was paying this cost

■ rent paid to a 'superior' landlord – this would apply only if the property did not belong to the client, but was rented from someone else, the situation would therefore be one of 'subletting'

■ interest paid on a loan or mortgage to buy the property – this applies where the client is the owner; where payments are made to the lender that include both interest and repayment of the amount borrowed, only the interest part is allowable

- insurance and management expenses

- costs of advertising for tenants

- ongoing repairs, maintenance and redecoration costs (but not those of a *capital* nature – see next page)

- irrecoverable rent (as discussed above)

- wear and tear allowance, if the property is rented out on a furnished basis

Expenditure that satisfies the above rules and is incurred before the premises are rented out or in periods in between rental periods ('void' periods) is also generally allowable. However such expenditure is not allowed during periods when the property is used privately - for example when a family member is living there without paying rent.

wear and tear allowance

For furnished residential lettings only, **wear and tear allowance** is a reflection of the costs involved in providing and maintaining suitable furniture and other items in the property. It is calculated as:

10% of the rent received (after deducting only rates (general and water) and council tax (where applicable) from the rent)

Wear and tear allowance is a broad measure that is easy to calculate and simply provides some recognition that costs are incurred in the provision of furniture. The logic for deducting rates or council tax before applying the 10% in the calculation is that the rent would have been artificially increased to cover them in the first place, since they are normally the tenant's responsibility. It would therefore be unfair to allow more wear and tear allowance just because the landlord was effectively collecting and paying out these amounts. Note that the calculation does not take account of how much the landlord spends on furniture, nor how he depreciates it in his accounts.

Where there is irrecoverable rent, this is deducted from the rent receivable before the 10% is applied.

Wear and tear allowance is normally claimed through the UK Property pages of the self assessment tax return, as we will see later in this chapter. However, the time limit for making the initial claim is one year after the 31 January following the end of the tax year – i.e. one year after the online return is due.

Wear and tear allowance cannot be claimed for holiday lets (see later in this chapter).

EXPENDITURE THAT IS NOT ALLOWABLE

Since only revenue expenditure is allowable, it follows that any capital expenditure will not be allowable. Non-allowable capital expenditure includes the following:

■ the **cost of the property itself** together with any furniture etc (unless renewals allowance is claimed). Also considered as capital will be the costs connected with the purchase, including the legal and professional fees and Stamp Duty Land Tax incurred in buying the property

■ the **cost of improvements**. This will apply when expenditure is incurred in upgrading or extending the property. For example, building a garage is an improvement, as is the installation of central heating where none existed previously. Note that normal ongoing repairs and maintenance when the property is simply brought back to its previous condition are allowable

■ the **cost of renovations** carried out before a property is rented out for the first time. One argument for viewing this expenditure as capital is that the need for the renovations will have been reflected in the lower purchase price of the property

Other costs that are not allowable include the following:

■ depreciation of any kind relating to capital expenditure

■ expenditure not connected with the business of lettings (for example, expenditure on a private part of the property)

CALCULATING THE PROFIT OR LOSS UNDER PROPERTY INCOME

To arrive at the profit or loss under property income we need to:

■ determine the assessable rents receivable, and

■ deduct any allowable expenditure

The calculation of the profit or loss is known as a **property income computation**.

dealing with a single property

We will now present a Case Study involving a single property to show how this calculation can be carried out. We will use the information regarding allowable expenditure to help us (see pages 2.3 and 2.4).

**Case
Study**

UNA LODGE:
CALCULATING ASSESSABLE PROPERTY INCOME

Una Lodge rents out one furnished property. The following is a statement compiled from her accounting records relating to the period 6/4/2014 - 5/4/2015.

	£	£
Rental Income Receivable		12,000
less expenditure:		
Council Tax	800	
Water Rates	400	
Irrecoverable Rent	600	
Insurance	300	
Installing Central Heating	2,000	
Depreciation of Furniture	900	
Managing Agent's Charges	600	
		5,600
Profit		6,400

required

Calculate the assessable property income for Una Lodge.

solution

We can re-draft the profit statement, incorporating only allowable expenditure and deductions as follows:

Property Income Computation

	£	£
Rental Income		12,000
less allowable expenditure:		
Council Tax	800	
Water Rates	400	
Irrecoverable Rent	600	
Insurance	300	
Managing Agent's Charges	600	
Wear & Tear Allowance	1,020	
		3,720
Assessable		8,280

Notes

- The installation of central heating is capital expenditure, and therefore not allowable for tax purposes.
- Depreciation is never allowable.
- The wear and tear allowance is calculated as: 10% x (£12,000 - £600 irrecoverable rent - £800 council tax - £400 water rates) = £1,020.

several properties

When there is more than one property, the best approach is to draw up a statement with one column for each property. The addition of a total column provides a means of double-checking your arithmetic, and sets out the figures needed for the tax return. Each property can then be dealt with in turn, and the overall result incorporated into one property income assessment figure. If one property then incurs a loss after adjustment for tax purposes, it should be offset against the assessable profits from the other properties. Using a columnar format like this enables the net result to be calculated quite easily, as in the Case Study which follows.

In a later section (page 2.13) we will go on to see how to deal with a situation where the net effect of all the properties is a loss.

Case Study

ANDY LORD:
PROFITS FROM SEVERAL PROPERTIES

Andy Lord rents out three properties in High Street. Property number 1 is unfurnished, while properties 2 and 3 are furnished.

Andy has provided the following statement of income and expenditure on the properties for the period 6/4/2014 - 5/4/2015.

	Property 1		Property 2		Property 3	
	£	£	£	£	£	£
Rental Income		5,000		3,500		4,300
Less expenses:						
Council Tax	500		-		400	
Loan Interest	3,600		2,040		-	
Rent Payable	-		-		2,500	
Property Insurance	200		200		200	
Bad Debt	600		-		-	
Roof Repairs	700		-		-	
Other Repairs	2,900		450		200	
Professional Fees						
for Debt Recovery	150		-		-	
Depreciation	500		500		500	
		9,150		3,190		3,800
Profit / (Loss)		(4,150)		310		500

You have also determined the following facts:

- property number two was occupied rent-free by Andy's student son until 5 September, when it was let out commercially to a tenant. The repairs were completed in December. The other expenses relate to the whole tax year

- the loan interest relates to mortgages obtained to purchase properties number one and two

- the rent payable relates to property number three that is not owned by Andy Lord

- the bad debt and the professional fees for attempted debt recovery relate to a problem with a tenant for property number one who left whilst owing rent. He cannot be traced

- 'Roof Repairs' relates to the cost of repairing damage that occurred during a storm. This amount was not covered by the insurance policy

- 'Other Repairs' includes £2,900 paid to build a porch on property number one

required

Calculate the amount of assessable property income.

solution

	Property 1	Property 2	Property 3	Total
	£	£	£	£
Rental Income	5,000	3,500	4,300	12,800
Less allowable expenses:				
Council Tax	500	-	400	900
Loan Interest	3,600	1,190	-	4,790
Rent Payable	-	-	2,500	2,500
Property Insurance	200	117	200	517
Bad Debt	600		-	600
Roof Repairs	700	-	-	700
Other Repairs	-	450	200	650
Professional Fees for Debt Recovery	150	-	-	150
Wear & Tear Allowance	-	350	390	740
Assessable amount	(750)	1,393	610	1,253

Notes

• Property number two is only rented out commercially for seven months of the tax year. Therefore only 7/12 of the loan interest and 7/12 of the property insurance expenses are allowable.

• The bad debt for property No. 1 is considered as irrecoverable rent and is therefore allowable.

• The professional fees for attempting to recover the debt are wholly and exclusively for the rental business and therefore allowable.

• The roof repairs are allowable as revenue expenditure.

• The 'other repairs' are allowable, with the exception of the porch that is considered an improvement and therefore capital in nature.

• Depreciation is not allowable.

• The wear and tear allowance is calculated as 10% of the rent less council tax. There is no wear and tear allowance for property No.1, since it is let unfurnished.

• The loss for property No. 1 is offset against the profits on the other properties to give a 'property income' figure of £1,253.

RENT A ROOM RELIEF

So far we have examined the situation where a taxpayer rents out a property that they are not currently living in. Where a part of an individual's own home is let out on a furnished basis, then a special relief, called 'rent a room relief' can be claimed. This can apply whether the individual owns or rents their home.

The relief means that gross income (ie before expenses) of up to £4,250 would be tax free for an individual. If the letting is carried out by a married couple or civil partnership in their home, then the relief is split so that each person's relief is £2,125.

The relief can apply to (for example)

■ renting out a spare room to a lodger, or

■ offering bed and breakfast

---

example

If a married couple rent out their spare room to a lodger for £80 per week for the whole year, their combined gross income from this would be £80 x 52 weeks = £4,160. Each individual's share of the gross income would be £2,080, and therefore each could claim that their income from this source was tax free.

If goods or services (for example food and / or laundry services) are provided in addition to the amount received just for the room, then the gross income relates to the combined amount receivable. This could apply to lodgers, or to a guest house or bed and breakfast operation.

example

An individual offers bed and breakfast for £40 per night per person during the summer months. If the room(s) are used for 100 guest-nights he will have gross income £40 x 100 = £4,000. Therefore rent a room relief can be claimed, and as the total income is less that £4,250 it will all be tax free.

Where the gross income is more than £4,250 per year, then the taxpayer has a choice:

■ they can claim rent a room relief which would mean that only the excess of gross income over £4,250 would be taxable (but no expenses could be claimed), or

■ they can ignore rent a room relief and calculate their profits from renting in the normal way by deducting allowable expenses

It would clearly make sense to choose the method that involves the lowest taxable amount!

The time limit for making an election regarding whether rent a room relief is claimed is one year after the 31 January following the end of the tax year – i.e. one year after the online return is due.

example

An individual rents out furnished rooms in his house for a total of £7,000 per year. His allowable expenses based on apportioned heating, lighting and insurance costs amounts to £1,500 per year.

He could claim rent a room relief, and be taxed on £7,000 – £4,250 = £2,750.

Alternatively he could elect to ignore rent a room relief and he would then be taxed on his rental profits calculated as follows:

	£
Gross Income	7,000
less wear and tear allowance	(700)
less other allowable expenses	(1,500)
Rental profit	4,800

In this situation it is better to claim rent a room relief. Note that if rent a room relief is claimed no other deductions can be claimed (not even wear and tear allowance).

PIERS SOUTH:
RENT A ROOM RELIEF

Piers South lets out part of his home during the holiday season. He lives in part of the building and uses the whole of the first floor for guest accommodation. He charges £50 per guest per night (including breakfast), and in the current tax year let out rooms for 250 guest-nights.

His expenses for the whole building were:

	£
Heating and lighting	2,000
Insurance	500
Mortgage interest	1,800

In addition he spent £1,300 on guests' breakfast food, £500 on laundering guest's bedding, and £1,000 employing a part time cleaner for the guest rooms.

The guest accommodation is 40% of the building, and this has been agreed as an appropriate way to apportion relevant costs.

Note that this situation qualifies as 'furnished holiday lettings' (see next section) and therefore wear and tear allowance cannot be claimed.

required

Calculate the amounts that would be subject to income tax if either

(a) rent a room relief was claimed, or

(b) normal rental profit calculations were carried out

Recommend whether rent a room relief should be claimed for this tax year.

solution

(a) claiming rent a room relief

	£
Gross Income (250 x £50)	12,500
Rent a room relief	(4,250)
Assessable amount	8,250

(b)   normal profit calculation

		£
Gross Income (250 x £50)		12,500
less:		
Breakfast food		(1,300)
Laundry expenses		(500)
Cleaner		(1,000)
Apportioned costs:		
Heating and lighting	(2,000 x 40%)	(800)
Insurance	(500 x 40%)	(200)
Mortgage interest	(1,800 x 40%)	(720)
Assessable amount		7,980

It is therefore better for Piers to use a normal profit calculation, and not claim rent a room relief in this case.

HOLIDAY LETS

We used an example of 'holiday lets' in the last case study, and you can see that when the normal profit calculation is used the rules are generally the same as for other property lettings. However, the calculation of the profit or loss on all holiday lets must be kept separate from other property rental.

The following are some of the main income tax points about holiday lets or 'furnished holiday lettings' as they are sometimes known:

■ holiday lets are eligible for rent a room relief if they are part of the individual's main home (as we have already seen)

■ mortgage interest can be claimed, except for the private part of a building

■ although wear and tear allowance cannot be claimed for holiday lets, capital allowances can be claimed on (for example) furniture and equipment (we don't need to consider the calculation of capital allowances for this study area)

■ pension contributions can be claimed in respect of the income from holiday lets (in a similar way to employment income – see Chapter 4)

■ a different page on the tax return is completed for holiday lets

Holiday lets could apply to (for example):

■ bed and breakfast lettings

■ holiday cottages that are rented out

■ caravans that are rented out

To qualify as a holiday let, the operation must be carried out commercially – with a view to making a profit. Letting out a taxpayer's own holiday home just to help with costs would not qualify. In addition, the accommodation must be available for public letting for at least 210 days a year, and be actually let for at least 105 days.

To qualify as a holiday let, the same tenant would not normally occupy the property for a continuous period of more than 31 days.

DEALING WITH PROPERTY LOSSES

Earlier in this chapter we saw how a loss when renting one property is offset against profits for other properties in the same tax year, provided they are of a similar type, ie holiday let or non-holiday let.

However, if *either*

■ there are no other properties with profits in that tax year, *or*

■ the net result from all the properties is a loss

then the following occurs:

■ the property income assessment for the tax year is nil, and

■ the loss must be carried forward until there is sufficient future property income to offset it

The property loss can only be set against future property income. If there are insufficient property income profits in the tax year that follows the loss, then the balance of the loss is carried forward again until it can be relieved.

If the loss relates to a holiday let, then it must be kept separate and relieved only against a profit from other holday lets.

The Case Study on the next page demonstrates how property losses are relieved.

Case Study

IVOR COST:
DEALING WITH LOSSES

Ivor Cost rents out several properties. None of these are holiday lets. After amalgamating the rents from all his properties, and deducting all allowable expenses he has arrived at the following figures:

Tax Year	Profit / (Loss)
	£
2012/13	(5,500)
2013/14	3,800
2014/15	6,400

required

Calculate the assessable property income for each of the three tax years referred to.

solution

Tax Year	Working	Property Income Assessment
2012/13	loss of £5,500 carried forward to next year	Nil
2013/14	£3,800 of loss used against profit of £3,800. Balance of loss carried forward	Nil
2014/15	Profit £6,400 less balance of loss £1,700	£4,700

COMPLETING THE RELEVANT PARTS OF THE TAX RETURN

In the first chapter we saw that a tax return consists of a main section that is common to all taxpayers, plus 'supplementary pages' that relate to specific situations. Details of property income or losses are entered on the supplementary pages that we will look at now.

These two pages are headed 'UK Property'. The first page, UKP 1 has a brief section for general information. This includes box 4 which is crossed if rent a room relief is claimed for gross income under the limit.

The remainder of the first page relates to furnished holiday lettings (holiday lets). The boxes are fairly self-explanatory. Be careful to only complete these sections if the letting qualifies as a holiday let. The profit or loss on furnished holiday lettings is recorded on page UKP1 quite separately from other property income. Normal lettings (furnished or unfurnished) are completed on the second page, UKP 2. We will now see how to complete this second page (which is the more complicated of the two and more likely to be tested).

The page broadly follows the format of a property income computation, with sections for:

- property income,
- property expenses, and
- calculating your taxable profit or loss

Since the tax form is designed to deal with more complicated situations than we need to study, you will find that we will not need some of the boxes. It is quite acceptable to leave boxes blank that do not apply.

Each box on the form is numbered for reference, and the notes that follow should help you understand how the form works.

Further guidance is available from the 'Notes on UK Property' document (SA105) that can be found on the HM Revenue & Customs website (www.hmrc.gov.uk), but note that such documents cannot be used in an examination.

The following sections are on page UKP2 of the tax form (see page 2.17 for the 2013/14 version)

'Property Income' Section

Here you will only need to complete box 20 with the rent receivable. This **excludes** any holiday letting income or profits that are shown on page UKP1.

'Property Expenses' Section

You should analyse the expenses (excluding any wear and tear allowance) into boxes 24 to 29. Make sure that the figures reconcile with your workings.

'Calculating your taxable profit or loss' Section

If there is any wear and tear allowance, this is inserted into box 36. If you are claiming rent a room relief against gross income, this is inserted into box 37, but you cannot also claim any expenses. The adjusted profit for the year that you have calculated is inserted into box 38.

Any loss brought forward from normal lettings is then entered into box 39 and the resulting taxable profit is entered in box 40. If there is a loss to be carried forward this is shown in boxes 41 and 43 (and then box 40 must be nil).

Once you have finished filling in this page, make sure that the figures agree with your earlier workings, and that the arithmetic is accurate.

 **HM Revenue & Customs**

UK property

Tax year 6 April 2013 to 5 April 2014

Your name

Your Unique Taxpayer Reference (UTR)

ℹ To get notes and helpsheets that will help you fill in this form, go to hmrc.gov.uk/selfassessmentforms

UK property details

1 Number of properties rented out

2 If all property income ceased in 2013–14 and you do not expect to receive such income in 2014–15, put 'X' in the box and consider if you need to fill in the *Capital gains summary* page

3 If you have any income from property let jointly, put 'X' in the box

4 If you are claiming Rent a Room relief and your rents are £4,250 or less (or £2,125 if let jointly), put 'X' in the box

Furnished holiday lettings (FHL) in the UK or European Economic Area (EEA)

Please read the **UK property notes** before filling in boxes 5 to 19. You need to fill in one page for UK businesses and a separate page for EEA businesses.

5 Income - *the amount of rent and any income for services provided to tenants*

£ . 0 0

6 Rent paid, repairs, insurance and costs of services provided - *the total amount*

£ . 0 0

7 Loan interest and other financial costs

£ . 0 0

8 Legal, management and other professional fees

£ . 0 0

9 Other allowable property expenses

£ . 0 0

10 Private use adjustment - *if expenses include any amounts for non-business purposes*

£ . 0 0

11 Balancing charges - *read the notes*

£ . 0 0

12 Capital allowances - *read the notes*

£ . 0 0

13 Adjusted profit for the year (if the amount in box 5 + box 10 + box 11 minus (boxes 6 to 9 + box 12) is positive)

£ . 0 0

14 Loss brought forward used against this year's profits - *if you have a non-FHL property business loss read the notes on property losses*

£ . 0 0

15 Taxable profit for the year (box 13 minus box 14)

£ . 0 0

16 Loss for the year (if the amount in boxes 6 to 9 + box 12 minus (box 5 + box 10 + box 11) is positive)

£ . 0 0

17 Total loss to carry forward

£ . 0 0

18 If this business is in the EEA, put 'X' in the box - *read the notes*

19 If you want to make a period of grace election, put 'X' in the box

Property income

Do not include furnished holiday lettings, Real Estate Investment Trust or Property Authorised Investment Funds dividends/distributions here.

20 Total rents and other income from property

£ [   ] . 0 0

21 Tax taken off any income in box 20 - *read the notes*

£ [   ] . 0 0

22 Premiums for the grant of a lease – from box E on the Working Sheet - *read the notes*

£ [   ] . 0 0

23 Reverse premiums and inducements

£ [   ] . 0 0

Property expenses

24 Rent, rates, insurance, ground rents etc.

£ [   ] . 0 0

25 Property repairs and maintenance

£ [   ] . 0 0

26 Loan interest and other financial costs

£ [   ] . 0 0

27 Legal, management and other professional fees

£ [   ] . 0 0

28 Costs of services provided, including wages

£ [   ] . 0 0

29 Other allowable property expenses

£ [   ] . 0 0

Calculating your taxable profit or loss

30 Private use adjustment - *read the notes*

£ [   ] . 0 0

31 Balancing charges - *read the notes*

£ [   ] . 0 0

32 Annual Investment Allowance

£ [   ] . 0 0

33 Business Premises Renovation Allowance (Assisted Areas only) - *read the notes*

£ [   ] . 0 0

34 All other capital allowances

£ [   ] . 0 0

35 Landlord's Energy Saving Allowance

£ [   ] . 0 0

36 10% wear and tear allowance - *for furnished residential accommodation only*

£ [   ] . 0 0

37 Rent a Room exempt amount

£ [   ] . 0 0

38 Adjusted profit for the year – from box O on the Working Sheet - *read the notes*

£ [   ] . 0 0

39 Loss brought forward used against this year's profits

£ [   ] . 0 0

40 Taxable profit for the year (box 38 minus box 39)

£ [   ] . 0 0

41 Adjusted loss for the year – from box O on the Working Sheet - *read the notes*

£ [   ] . 0 0

42 Loss set off against 2013-14 total income - *this will be unusual - read the notes*

£ [   ] . 0 0

43 Loss to carry forward to following year, including unused losses brought forward

£ [   ] . 0 0

We will now see how a completed page looks by using the data from the earlier Case Study 'Andy Lord'.

ANDY LORD:
COMPLETING THE RELEVANT TAX RETURN PAGES

Andy Lord rents out three properties in High Street. Two of the properties are furnished. The following is a computation of his property income (using the total column taken from the solution to the Case Study on page 2.8).

	£	£
Rental Income		12,800
less allowable expenses:		
Council Tax	900	
Loan Interest	4,790	
Rent Payable	2,500	
Property Insurance	517	
Bad Debt	600	
Roof Repairs	700	
Other Repairs	650	
Professional Fees for Debt Recovery	150	
Wear & Tear Allowance	740	
		11,547
Assessable amount		1,253

required
Complete page UKP2 of the tax return for Andy Lord.

solution
The completed document is reproduced on the opposite page. The following workings explain how each figure reconciles with the property income computation. *Note that we have used the 2013/14 form here, as the 2014/15 version is not available at the time of going to press.*

Box No. Workings and Comments

20   Rental Income (before any deductions) £12,800.

24   Council Tax £900 + Rent Payment £2,500 + Property Insurance £517 = £3,917.

25   Roof Repairs £700 + Other Repairs £650 = £1,350.

26   Loan Interest £4,790.

27   Professional Fees for Debt Recovery £150.

29   Bad Debt £600.

36   Wear & Tear Allowance £740.

38   The assessable profit for this year of £1,253.

40   The figure from box 38 repeated (since there are no losses brought forward in this case).

Property income

Do not include furnished holiday lettings, Real Estate Investment Trust or Property Authorised Investment Funds dividends/distributions here.

20 Total rents and other income from property

£ 1 2 8 0 0 · 0 0

21 Tax taken off any income in box 20 – *read the notes*

£ · 0 0

22 Premiums for the grant of a lease – from box E on the Working Sheet – *read the notes*

£ · 0 0

23 Reverse premiums and inducements

£ · 0 0

Property expenses

24 Rent, rates, insurance, ground rents etc.

£ 3 9 1 7 · 0 0

25 Property repairs and maintenance

£ 1 3 5 0 · 0 0

26 Loan interest and other financial costs

£ 4 7 9 0 · 0 0

27 Legal, management and other professional fees

£ 1 5 0 · 0 0

28 Costs of services provided, including wages

£ · 0 0

29 Other allowable property expenses

£ 6 0 0 · 0 0

Calculating your taxable profit or loss

30 Private use adjustment – *read the notes*

£ · 0 0

31 Balancing charges – *read the notes*

£ · 0 0

32 Annual Investment Allowance

£ · 0 0

33 Business Premises Renovation Allowance (Assisted Areas only) – *read the notes*

£ · 0 0

34 All other capital allowances

£ · 0 0

35 Landlord's Energy Saving Allowance

£ · 0 0

36 10% wear and tear allowance – *for furnished residential accommodation only*

£ 7 4 0 · 0 0

37 Rent a Room exempt amount

£ · 0 0

38 Adjusted profit for the year – from box O on the Working Sheet – *read the notes*

£ 1 2 5 3 · 0 0

39 Loss brought forward used against this year's profits

£ · 0 0

40 Taxable profit for the year (box 38 minus box 39)

£ 1 2 5 3 · 0 0

41 Adjusted loss for the year – from box O on the Working Sheet – *read the notes*

£ · 0 0

42 Loss set off against 2013-14 total income – *this will be unusual – read the notes*

£ · 0 0

43 Loss to carry forward to following year, including unused losses brought forward

£ · 0 0

To ensure that we can also complete the return for a holiday lets business, we will now use the data from our earlier case study 'Piers South' to illustrate completion of the return.

Case Study

PIERS SOUTH:
COMPLETING TAX RETURN UK PROPERTY PAGES

Piers South lets out part of his home during the holiday season. It qualifies as a furnished holiday lettings business. He has already calculated his assessable property income, and decided that it is beneficial not to claim rent a room relief, but instead to claim allowable expenses.

His calculation of assessable profit is as follows:

		£
Gross Income (250 x £50)		12,500
less:		
Breakfast food		(1,300)
Laundry expenses		(500)
Cleaner		(1,000)
Apportioned costs:		
Heating and lighting	(2,000 x 40%)	(800)
Insurance	(500 x 40%)	(200)
Mortgage interest	(1,800 x 40%)	(720)
Assessable amount		7,980

required

Complete the relevant parts of the property income pages for the business.

solution

The completed form is shown on the next page. We have used the 2013/14 version.

These notes will explain how it has been filled in.

Page UKP 1 is the only page required here

Box 5 shows the income of £12,500.

Box 6 shows the total of all the costs except mortgage interest. These costs have been treated as ' costs of services provided', although some could arguably have been inserted in box 9 as 'other allowable property expenses'.

Box 7 shows the mortgage interest.

Box 10 is left blank since the private use adjustments for 60% of the building expenses have already been deducted in the calculation of the amounts shown in boxes 6 and 7.

Box 13 is a profit sub total, and the figure is repeated in box 15 as there is no loss brought forward.

HM Revenue & Customs

UK property
Tax year 6 April 2013 to 5 April 2014

Your name

PIERS SOUTH

Your Unique Taxpayer Reference (UTR)

ⓘ To get notes and helpsheets that will help you fill in this form, go to hmrc.gov.uk/selfassessmentforms

UK property details

1 Number of properties rented out

1

2 If all property income ceased in 2013–14 and you do not expect to receive such income in 2014–15, put 'X' in the box and consider if you need to fill in the *Capital gains summary* page

3 If you have any income from property let jointly, put 'X' in the box

4 If you are claiming Rent a Room relief and your rents are £4,250 or less (or £2,125 if let jointly), put 'X' in the box

Furnished holiday lettings (FHL) in the UK or European Economic Area (EEA)

Please read the **UK property notes** before filling in boxes 5 to 19. You need to fill in one page for UK businesses and a separate page for EEA businesses.

5 Income - *the amount of rent and any income for services provided to tenants*

£ 12500 . 00

6 Rent paid, repairs, insurance and costs of services provided - *the total amount*

£ 3800 . 00

7 Loan interest and other financial costs

£ 720 . 00

8 Legal, management and other professional fees

£ . 00

9 Other allowable property expenses

£ . 00

10 Private use adjustment - *if expenses include any amounts for non-business purposes*

£ . 00

11 Balancing charges - *read the notes*

£ . 00

12 Capital allowances - *read the notes*

£ . 00

13 Adjusted profit for the year (if the amount in box 5 + box 10 + box 11 minus (boxes 6 to 9 + box 12) is positive)

£ 7980 . 00

14 Loss brought forward used against this year's profits - *if you have a non-FHL property business loss read the notes on property losses*

£ . 00

15 Taxable profit for the year (box 13 minus box 14)

£ 7980 . 00

16 Loss for the year (if the amount in boxes 6 to 9 + box 12 minus (box 5 + box 10 + box 11) is positive)

£ . 00

17 Total loss to carry forward

£ . 00

18 If this business is in the EEA, put 'X' in the box - *read the notes*

19 If you want to make a period of grace election, put 'X' in the box

KEEPING RECORDS

Records for property income must normally be kept for five years after the online tax return is due to be submitted. For the tax year 2014/15 the return is due on 31 January 2016, and so the records must be kept until 31 January 2021. Note that this is longer than non-business records need to be kept for tax purposes (one year after the final online tax return submission date).

The records should be able to substantiate the entries on the tax return, and would therefore typically include:

- accounting records including cash books and bank statements
- rental agreements and other records of tenancies
- invoices or receipts for expenses paid
- working papers for computations
- copies of tax returns

Chapter Summary

- Income from renting land and property is assessed under 'property income'. The basis of assessment for this is the income relating to the tax year, less allowable expenses, calculated on an accruals basis. The calculation of the assessable amount is known as a property income computation.

- Allowable expenses are those wholly and exclusively for the business of lettings. Irrecoverable rent is an allowable expense, as is a 'wear and tear allowance' for residential property that is let furnished.

- Expenditure that is not allowable includes capital expenditure and any form of depreciation.

- Where more than one property is let, the results are combined and any individual losses netted off against other properties with profits. Where the overall result is a loss, this is carried forward against future property income profits. Losses for furnished holiday lettings can only be offset against profits from furnished holiday lettings. Similarly, non-holiday letting losses can only be offset against non-holiday letting profits.

- Rent a room relief can apply where furnished accommodation is provided in a taxpayer's main home. It can exempt up to £4,250 of gross income.

- There are supplementary pages in the tax return that relate to UK property. These must be completed accurately and agree with the computation. The relevant records must be retained for five years after the submission date for the online tax return.

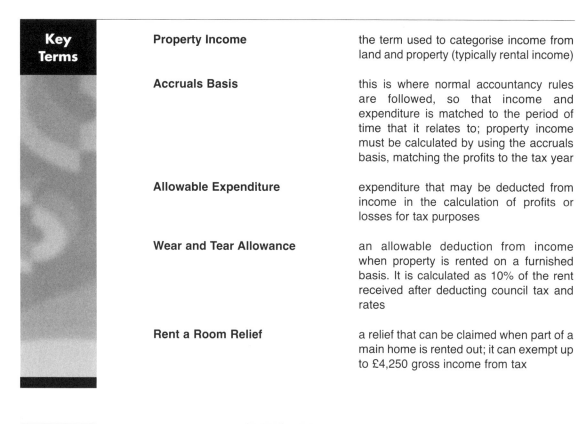

Key Terms		
	Property Income	the term used to categorise income from land and property (typically rental income)
	Accruals Basis	this is where normal accountancy rules are followed, so that income and expenditure is matched to the period of time that it relates to; property income must be calculated by using the accruals basis, matching the profits to the tax year
	Allowable Expenditure	expenditure that may be deducted from income in the calculation of profits or losses for tax purposes
	Wear and Tear Allowance	an allowable deduction from income when property is rented on a furnished basis. It is calculated as 10% of the rent received after deducting council tax and rates
	Rent a Room Relief	a relief that can be claimed when part of a main home is rented out; it can exempt up to £4,250 gross income from tax

Activities

2.1 Julie rented out her unfurnished property from 6/7/2014, and received £5,000 for 12 month's rent in advance on that day. She also set up a direct debit payment of £25 per month for property insurance. In December 2014 she spent £200 for repairs following a burst pipe.

Calculate the assessable property income for 2014/15.

2.2 Dave bought an unfurnished office on 6/11/2014, and immediately let it to a tenant for £400 per month, payable monthly. Dave paid £2,000 legal fees to acquire the office, and paid monthly mortgage interest relating to the office of £150. He also paid £30 per month property insurance.

Dave used the services of an agent to collect the rent and liaise with the tenant. The agent charged £1,200 per year for this service.

Calculate the assessable property income for 2014/15.

2.3   Anna Partement rents out one furnished property. The following is a statement compiled from her accounting records relating to the tax year:

	£	£
Rental Income Receivable		10,000
less expenditure:		
Council Tax	700	
Water Rates	300	
Insurance	400	
Cost of New Carpets	2,500	
Depreciation of Furniture	800	
Managing Agent's Charges	1,000	
		5,700
Profit		4,300

Required:

Calculate the property income for Anna for the tax year.

2.4   Sonny Hill rents out three country cottages. All properties are furnished.

He has provided the following statement of income and expenditure on the properties for the tax year:

	Property 1		Property 2		Property 3	
	£	£	£	£	£	£
Rental Income		8,000		6,000		5,500
Less expenses:						
Council Tax	800		650		400	
Loan Interest	3,600		2,000		4,000	
Property Insurance	400		300		250	
Redecoration	-		600		-	
Repainting Windows	500		450		500	
Other Repairs	2,900		400		200	
Accountancy Fees	150		150		150	
Depreciation	500		500		500	
		8,850		5,050		6,000
Profit / (Loss)		(850)		950		(500)

You have also determined the following facts:

• property number three was purchased on 6 June. This property was rented out from 6 July. The council tax on this property relates to the nine month period from 6 July. Other expenses relate to the ten month period from 6 June

• the loan interest relates to mortgages obtained to purchase the properties

• 'Other Repairs' includes £2,600 paid to install central heating in property number one where none had previously existed

• Sonny Hill has an unrelieved property income loss of £1,000 brought forward from the previous tax year

Required:

1   Calculate the property income for the tax year.

2   Complete the blank supplementary page from the tax return (see next page for the 2013/14 version).

2.5   Maisey Nett rents out one furnished property. The following is a statement compiled from her accounting records relating to the tax year.

	£	£
Rental Income Receivable		11,500
less expenditure:		
Accountancy Fees	400	
Council Tax	650	
Water Rates	350	
Insurance	300	
Cost of New Furniture	2,000	
Mortgage Interest	2,300	
Managing Agent's Charges	1,000	
		7,000
Profit		4,500

Maisey also had gross income of £41,500 in the tax year from her job as a legal executive. She paid £6,300 income tax under PAYE.

Required:

1   Calculate the property income for Maisey.

2   Calculate Maisey's total income tax liability for the tax year, and the part of that amount that she has yet to pay.

Property income

Do not include furnished holiday lettings, Real Estate Investment Trust or Property Authorised Investment Funds dividends/ distributions here.

20 **Total rents and other income from property**

£ _____ · 0 0

21 **Tax taken off any income in box 20** - *read the notes*

£ _____ · 0 0

22 **Premiums for the grant of a lease – from box E on the Working Sheet** - *read the notes*

£ _____ · 0 0

23 **Reverse premiums and inducements**

£ _____ · 0 0

Property expenses

24 **Rent, rates, insurance, ground rents etc.**

£ _____ · 0 0

25 **Property repairs and maintenance**

£ _____ · 0 0

26 **Loan interest and other financial costs**

£ _____ · 0 0

27 **Legal, management and other professional fees**

£ _____ · 0 0

28 **Costs of services provided, including wages**

£ _____ · 0 0

29 **Other allowable property expenses**

£ _____ · 0 0

Calculating your taxable profit or loss

30 **Private use adjustment** - *read the notes*

£ _____ · 0 0

31 **Balancing charges** - *read the notes*

£ _____ · 0 0

32 **Annual Investment Allowance**

£ _____ · 0 0

33 **Business Premises Renovation Allowance (Assisted Areas only)** - *read the notes*

£ _____ · 0 0

34 **All other capital allowances**

£ _____ · 0 0

35 **Landlord's Energy Saving Allowance**

£ _____ · 0 0

36 **10% wear and tear allowance** - *for furnished residential accommodation only*

£ _____ · 0 0

37 **Rent a Room exempt amount**

£ _____ · 0 0

38 **Adjusted profit for the year – from box O on the Working Sheet** - *read the notes*

£ _____ · 0 0

39 **Loss brought forward used against this year's profits**

£ _____ · 0 0

40 **Taxable profit for the year (box 38 minus box 39)**

£ _____ · 0 0

41 **Adjusted loss for the year – from box O on the Working Sheet** - *read the notes*

£ _____ · 0 0

42 **Loss set off against 2013–14 total income** - *this will be unusual – read the notes*

£ _____ · 0 0

43 **Loss to carry forward to following year, including unused losses brought forward**

£ _____ · 0 0

2.6   Simon has two properties in addition to his home, details of which are as follows:

Three bedroom house:

(1)   This unfurnished house is rented out for £900 per month. The property was occupied this tax year until 1 September when the tenants suddenly moved out, owing the rent for July and August. Simon knows that he will not recover this rent. The property was let again from 1 December to another family.

(2)   The only expense paid by Simon on the house was 8% management charge to the agent on rent received.

One bedroom flat:

(3)   This furnished flat is rented out for £450 per month. The property was unoccupied this tax year until 1 June when a couple moved in on a twelve month lease.

(4)   Simon paid council tax and water rates on the flat, totalling £1,400 for the period that the flat was occupied. He also paid insurance of £270 for the year.

Calculate the profit or loss made on each property, using the following table.

	Three bedroom house £	**One bedroom flat** £
Income		
Expenses:		

2.7   Select the statements that are true from the following:

(a)   The maximum amount of gross rent that can be received tax free under the rent a room scheme is £4,250.

(b)   The rent a room scheme applies to unfurnished accommodation.

(c)   Rent a room relief cannot be claimed for guest houses.

(d)   Taxpayers cannot claim both rent a room relief and wear and tear allowance for the same property.

(e)   If the gross rent receivable is over £4,250 taxpayers can choose whether to claim rent a room relief or use a standard profit calculation.

(f)   If you live in rented accommodation you cannot claim rent a room relief.

(g)   Charges for goods or services like food or laundry are included when calculating the gross rent.

for your notes

3 Income from savings and investments

this chapter covers...

In this chapter we examine the way that savings and investment income is taxed. This includes interest from (for example) banks and building societies and dividends from shares in UK companies.

We will learn that assessment is based on the amount received (not the accruals basis), and that some (but not all) income is received after tax has been treated as deducted at source.

We will then go on to see how savings income and dividend income both have tax bands that are not quite the same as the bands for general income. The income needs to work through these bands in a specific order and this is explained and illustrated.

Next we summarise the sources of tax-free investment income. Finally we list typical records that should be kept and remind ourselves of the length of time that these must be retained for.

THE BASIS OF ASSESSMENT FOR SAVINGS AND INVESTMENT INCOME

In this chapter we will examine savings and investment income and see how it is taxed. There are two types of savings and investment income. They are:

■ interest received from various sources

■ dividends from shares held in limited companies

Examples from which interest is received are:

■ bank and building society deposit or savings accounts

■ government securities ('Gilts')

■ loans to local authorities

■ loans to limited companies (Debentures)

Examples of companies from which dividends are received are:

■ PLC's such as 'Marks and Spencer plc'

■ private limited companies such as 'Osborne Books Ltd'

The basis of assessment for both interest and UK dividends is the gross equivalent of the amount **received in the tax year**. Notice that this receipts basis applies to most types of income, but is different from property income which is calculated on an accruals basis. The period that the interest is based on is therefore irrelevant. Amounts received include money credited to an individual's bank or building society accounts during the tax year. There are no allowable expenses that can be deducted in the calculation of savings and investment income.

TAX DEDUCTED AT SOURCE

Most (but not all) of the savings and investment income that we will come across is received after some tax has effectively been deducted from the amount that will count as income. This works as follows:

■ interest is often received after 20% of the gross amount has been deducted

■ interest from some sources can be received as a gross amount without any deduction

■ dividends will always be received after a notional 10% 'tax credit' has been effectively deducted

Note that both percentages relate to the 'gross' amounts, and are not percentages of the amounts that are actually received. We will see in the next section how these percentages link into the tax rates that apply to these forms of income.

Tax deducted from interest received and tax credits on dividends have the same general effect – they are both treated as part of the individual's tax liability **that has already been paid**. In this way it is similar to tax deducted under PAYE. The main difference between tax credits and other tax deducted is that tax credits are not repayable if it turns out that the individual has paid too much income tax.

Apart from tax-free income, (which we will examine later in this chapter) it is always the gross amount that is assessable for tax purposes. This is irrespective of whether the investment income is received 'net' or 'gross'. The gross figure is therefore the amount included in the individual's income tax computation.

You will be expected to know the main sources of savings and investment income, and how to calculate the assessable amounts and any tax deduction or tax credits that apply. These details are outlined in the following table.

Type of Savings and Investment Income	Received	Tax Deduction
Interest from:		
Government Securities ('Gilts')	Gross	None
Bank & Building Society Accounts	Net	20%
Limited Company Loans	Net	20%
Local Authority Loans	Net	20%
Dividends from UK Company Shares	Net	10%

calculating the gross and tax amounts

We may be provided, on a tax voucher, for example, with a full analysis of the gross amount, the deduction and the net figure received.

For example, interest received of

Net Amount Received	£640.00	
Tax Deducted	£160.00	(20% of £800.00)
Gross Amount	£800.00	

or dividends received of:

Amount Received	£720.00	
Tax Credit	£80.00	(10% of £800.00)
Dividend + Tax Credit	£800.00	

Notice that the percentage deductions (20% for the interest and 10% for the dividends) both relate to the 'gross' figures. Many references do not use the term 'gross' in relation to dividends – the preferred expression is 'dividend plus tax credit'.

If we are only presented with the figures for the amounts received then (unless the income is received gross) we will need to calculate the tax deducted and gross amounts, as in the examples just given. This calculation is carried out as follows:

For **interest** that is received net, 20/80 of the net amount must be added for the tax deducted.

For **dividends**, 10/90 of the amount received must be added for the tax credit.

Alternatively, the assessable figure can be calculated by multiplying net interest by 100/80 and dividends by 100/90.

This diagram illustrates these principles:

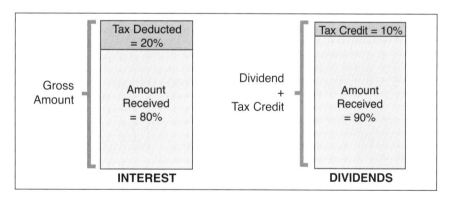

Using the interest example given above, the tax deducted could be calculated as 20/80 x £640.00 = £160.00. Added to the net amount of £640.00 this gives the gross figure of £800.00.

Similarly, the tax credit on the dividend can be worked out as £720.00 x 10/90 = £80.00.

election for non-taxpayers

Individuals who do not pay income tax because their total income is less than their personal allowance can elect to receive interest from a bank or building society gross. The election is made on form R85. Note, however, that this does not apply to dividends.

We will now use a Case Study to see how the principles studied so far in this chapter can be applied in practice.

ANNE INVESTOR:
CALCULATING SAVINGS AND DIVIDEND INCOME

Anne has provided you with the following details of the amounts that she has received during 2014 and part of 2015 from her various investments.

Date Received	Details	Amount Rec'd
		£
31/3/2014	Callifax Bank Deposit Account Interest	120.00
31/5/2014	Dividend from Gloxxo plc	13,500.00
30/6/2014	Newtown Building Society A/C Interest	1,200.00
31/8/2014	Dividend from CIC plc	6,750.00
30/9/2014	Interest from CIC plc Debenture	5,000.00
31/1/2015	Bank of Cambria Deposit A/C Interest	6,500.00
31/3/2015	Callifax Bank Deposit Account Interest	300.00
31/5/2015	Dividend from Gloxxo plc	9,000.00

required

Produce schedules of the amounts of savings and dividend income assessable in 2014/15, and the amounts of tax deducted at source and tax credits.

solution

1 The first step is to make sure that we only include amounts received between 6/4/2014 and 5/4/2015 in our calculation for 2014/15. This means that we can ignore the first Callifax interest of £120, and the last Gloxxo plc dividend of £9,000.

2 The second step is to categorise the receipts into savings and dividend income, and to produce schedules showing the amounts received, the tax deducted or tax credit, and the assessable amounts. We must be careful to check the source of each savings income to determine whether it will have been received net or gross. In this Case Study there are no amounts that are received gross.

This provides us with the following analysis.

SAVINGS INCOME

Date	Details	Amount Received	Tax Deducted	Assessable Amount
		£	£	£
30/6/14	Newtown BS	1,200.00	300.00	1,500.00
30/9/14	CIC Debenture	5,000.00	1,250.00	6,250.00
31/1/15	Bank of Cambria	6,500.00	1,625.00	8,125.00
31/3/15	Callifax Bank	300.00	75.00	375.00
Total		13,000.00	3,250.00	16,250.00

DIVIDEND INCOME

Date	Details	Amount Received	Tax Credit	Assessable Amount
		£	£	£
31/5/14	Gloxxo plc	13,500.00	1,500.00	15,000.00
31/8/14	CIC plc	6,750.00	750.00	7,500.00
Total		20,250.00	2,250.00	22,500.00

Remember that the assessable amounts would be included in Anne's tax computation for 2014/15, and the tax deducted and tax credits would be treated as payments of tax already made.

TAX BANDS AND RATES FOR SAVINGS AND DIVIDEND INCOME

Although the tax rates for general income are 20%, 40% and 45% (as we saw in the last chapters), the rates for savings and dividend income are not always the same as these. Instead savings income and dividend income each have their own tax rates that apply in the various tax bands.

Income from savings and dividends are the only exceptions to the general income tax rates that we saw in Chapter 1. We therefore have a total of three categories of income that have different tax rates:

- general income
- savings income, and
- dividend income

General income is any income except that from savings or dividends.

The following chart (which is not to scale) shows the tax bands and rates for these three types of income, and is based on the tax year 2014/15.

Tax bands and tax rates, 2014/15			
Additional Rate	45%	45%	37.5%
£150,000			
Higher Rate	40%	40%	32.5%
£31,865			
Basic Rate	20%	20%	10%
£2,880			
Starting Rate		10%	
£0			
	General Income	Savings Income	Dividend Income

You can see from the chart that there is a special 10% starting rate that applies to savings income in certain circumstances, even though there is no equivalent starting rate for general income or dividend income.

using the rates and bands

It is vital when working out an individual's tax that the taxable income is analysed into these three categories, and that this analysis is clearly shown in your answers to exam questions. A specific order is followed when calculating tax on each category of income. This order is:

- general income; then
- savings income; and finally
- dividend income

Dividend income is therefore considered the 'top slice' of an individual's taxable income, with savings income the middle slice.

Suppose someone has £47,000 taxable income (after deducting the personal allowance) made up as follows for the tax year 2014/15:

- general income   £15,000
- savings income   £12,000
- dividend income   £20,000

The bands would be worked through starting with the general income amounts and rates, then moving up through the savings income rates, and finally using the dividend income rates.

The band levels apply to the whole income, so each time we move into the next type of income we use the cumulative income to determine the rate. In our example, this would work as follows:

General Income	£15,000 x 20% (all at the basic rate)	= £3,000.00
Savings Income	£12,000 x 20% (all at the basic rate)	= £2,400.00
Dividend Income	£4,865 x 10% (up to £31,865 cumulative)	= £486.50
	£15,135 x 32.5% (the rest of the dividends)	= £4,918.87
Total tax liability		£10,805.37

The diagram on the next page (which is not to scale) illustrates how the system works, using the figures shown above. We have ignored the Additional Rate band in this diagram as the income is not high enough to use it. Notice how the bar representing each type of income starts at the level that the previous one ended. This is the key to understanding the system.

The personal allowance is deducted from the general income when analysing the taxable income. If there is insufficient general income to do this then the savings income is used, and finally dividend income.

The starting rate of 10% for savings income will only apply if the taxable general income is less than £2,880. In all situations where taxable general income is £2,880 or more the 10% starting rate for savings income will not apply. This is the position illustrated in the last example.

The starting rate of 10% for savings income will therefore only benefit taxpayers who have less than £2,880 of taxable general income.

Using the tax rates and bands, 2014/15

	General Income	Savings Income	Dividend Income
Higher Rate	40%	40%	32.5%
			£20,000
£31,865			
		£12,000	
Basic Rate	20%	20%	10%
	£15,000		
£2,880		10%	
Starting Rate			
£0			

To summarise:

- always work up the bands, following the order:
  - general income
  - savings income
  - dividend income
- always use the cumulative taxable income totals to determine the bands

We can now build on the last Case Study to look at a more comprehensive income tax computation.

This Case Study does not refer to or use the Additional Rate band, since the taxable income is below £150,000. In Chapter 5 we will see how this band is used and also the impact of the changes to the personal allowance for those with high incomes.

Case Study

ANNE INVESTOR: INCOME TAX COMPUTATION

Anne Investor has investment income for 2014/15 (see page 3.4) that has been summarised as follows:

Savings Income

	Amount Received £	Tax Deducted £	Assessable Amount £
Total	13,000.00	3,250.00	16,250.00

Dividend Income

	Amount Received £	Tax Credit £	Assessable Amount £
Total	20,250.00	2,250.00	22,500.00

Anne also has gross income from employment for 2014/15 of £7,000, from which nothing was deducted under PAYE. She is entitled to the normal personal allowance of £10,000.

required
Using an income tax computation, calculate the income tax liability for 2014/15, and the amount of tax that Anne has not yet paid.

solution

Income Tax Computation

	Income £	Tax already paid £
Employment Income	7,000	0
Savings income (as above)	16,250	3,250
Dividend income (as above)	22,500	2,250
Total Income	45,750	5,500
Less Personal Allowance	10,000	
Taxable Income	35,750	

Analysis of Taxable Income:

General Income	(lower than personal allowance)	£0
Savings Income	(16,250 − (10,000 − 7,000))	£13,250
Dividend Income		£22,500
		£35,750

Income Tax Calculation:

		£	£
Savings Income:			
£2,880 x 10%		288.00	
£10,370 x 20%	(£13,250 − £2,880)	2,074.00	
£13,250			2,362.00
Dividend Income:			
£18,615 x 10%	(£31,865 − £13,250)	1,861.50	
£3,885 x 32.5%	(the rest of £22,500)	1,262.62	
£22,500			3,124.12
	Income Tax Liability		5,486.12
	Less Paid		5,500.00
	Income Tax to be Refunded		(13.88)

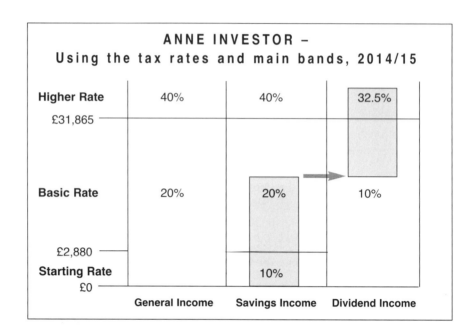

ANNE INVESTOR –
Using the tax rates and main bands, 2014/15

	General Income	Savings Income	Dividend Income
Higher Rate	40%	40%	32.5%
£31,865			
Basic Rate	20%	20%	10%
£2,880			
Starting Rate		10%	
£0			

ASSESSMENT SUMMARY

As you can see, the income tax computation in the Case Study is more complicated than the calculations that we saw in the earlier chapters. The way the tax is calculated for each category of income by working up through the bands is illustrated in the chart shown above. Make sure that you can follow the logic, since it is very important for your success in this Unit that you can carry out computations like this accurately.

TAX-FREE INVESTMENT INCOME

Some specific types of investment income are exempt from income tax. You may recall that this was referred to in Chapter 1. The implications of having tax-free investment income are that:

■ the tax-free income is not included in the income tax computation, and

■ the tax-free income is not recorded on the tax return

new individual savings accounts (NISAs)

You need to understand what new individual savings accounts (NISAs) are and how they operate. These accounts have replaced individual savings accounts (ISAs) from 1 July 2014 and provide income which is exempt from income tax. The accounts are also exempt from capital gains tax.

All existing ISAs automatically become NISAs on 1 July 2014, and the following rules for investment in these accounts then apply. Investment can be in 'stocks and shares' and/or 'cash' and are limited to a maximum total investment of £15,000 in 2014/15. There are no restrictions on how much can be invested in each category within this overall limit, and amounts invested in one category can subsequently be moved to the other (subject to the age of the individual – see below). This is much less restrictive than the limits and rules that applied to ISAs previously.

For example, £15,000 could be invested in a 'stocks and shares NISA' in July 2014, and subsequently all of it could be moved during the tax year to a 'cash NISA'. The same ability to move between cash and stocks and shares also applies in 2014/15 to investments made in ISAs before 2014/15.

There is no statutory minimum period of investment or amount of investment in any type of NISA.

NISAs can only be held in one person's name – joint accounts are not permitted.

Each individual can only put money into one cash ISA and one stocks and shares NISA in a tax year. However in different tax years, investment could be made with different providers. There are no limits on the number of different NISAs one can hold over time.

cash NISAs

Cash NISAs are effectively special accounts, mainly offered by banks or building societies. These accounts pay interest tax-free. Once an investment is made into a NISA the income remains tax free in subsequent tax years.

If a withdrawal is made from a cash NISA the amount cannot be reinvested without it counting as part of that year's maximum investment. Therefore if the maximum had already been invested the withdrawn amount could not be reinvested during that tax year.

Cash NISAs can be transferred to another provider (for example if interest rates are better), but this must be carried out by contacting the new provider who will organise the transfer. If an amount is simply withdrawn from an existing NISA account it will lose its tax-free status.

Investment in cash NISAs can be made by UK resident individuals who are aged 16 or over during the tax year.

stocks and shares NISAs

Stocks and shares NISAs are effectively tax-free 'wrappers' for investments including shares in listed companies and government securities (gilts).

Investment in stocks and shares NISAs can be made by UK resident individuals who are aged 18 or over.

KEEPING RECORDS

Records of savings and dividend income need to be kept approximately 22 months after the end of the tax year to which they relate. This means that 2014/15 records need to be retained until 31/01/17 – one year after the final submission date for the online tax return.

Typical records that should be retained include:

- interest statements or tax deduction certificates
- dividend vouchers
- account details
- working papers for investment income
- copies of tax returns

The first two items on this list would normally be provided automatically by the organisation making the payments.

Chapter Summary

- Interest and dividends are categorised as 'Savings and Investment Income'. The basis of assessment is the gross equivalent of the amounts received in the tax year. Most interest is received net of a 20% income tax deduction, although interest from some sources is received gross. Dividends are always received after a notional 10% tax credit has been deducted from the assessable amount.

- Savings income and dividend income are both taxed at different rates from general income. The rates for savings income are 10%, 20%, 40% and 45%, while the rates for dividend income are 10%, 32.5% and 37.5%. Dividend income is considered the top slice of an individual's income, with savings income forming the next slice. This means that great care must be taken when calculating an individual's tax liability if income of these types is included.

- Investment income from new individual savings accounts (NISAs) is exempt from income tax. There are various rules concerning investments in NISAs.

Key Terms

Savings and Investment income	the term used to describe income that arises from the ownership of certain assets, it can include savings income and dividend income
Government securities ('Gilts')	these are effectively loans to the UK government; although the interest on the investment is taxable, it is paid gross
Dividends	these are the rewards received by investors in company shares; the amount received is considered to be after a 10% 'tax credit' has been deducted
Tax Credit	this is a notional amount that recipients of dividends are deemed to have paid; it is similar in concept to income tax deducted at source, but is not repayable

Activities

3.1 Anna Mount received the following amounts from her investments during 2014/15:

Date Received	Details	Amount Received
30/6/14	Nat East Bank Interest	£1,600
30/9/14	Osborne plc Dividends	£2,700

Required:

Calculate the assessable amounts of savings and dividend income for 2014/15, and the associated amounts of tax deducted at source and tax credits.

3.2 Max Growth has provided you with the following details of the amounts that he has received during 2014/15 from his various investments.

Date Received	Details	Amount Rec'd
		£
31/5/2014	Dividend from PCR plc	1,440.00
30/6/2014	Oldport Building Society A/C Interest	1,680.00
30/9/2014	Interest from PCR plc Debenture	2,000.00
31/1/2015	Exchequer Stock (Gilt) Interest	6,500.00
31/3/2015	Premium Bond Prize	5,000.00

Required:

Produce schedules of the amounts of savings and dividend income assessable in 2014/15, and the amounts of tax deducted at source and tax credits.

3.3   Sophie had the following income in 2014/15:

Income from Employment (gross amount)	£28,500
Building Society Interest (net amount received)	£1,200
Dividends from UK Companies (amount received)	£3,600
Property Income (agreed assessable amount)	£1,900

Sophie had income tax deducted under PAYE of £3,700. She is entitled to the normal personal allowance of £10,000.

Required:

Prepare Sophie's Income Tax Computation for the tax year, including calculations of her total income tax liability, and the part of this amount that has yet to be paid.

3.4   Brian had the following income in 2014/15:

Salary of £1,800 per month (gross) from his employment.	
Dividends from UK companies (amount received)	£2,700
Bank Deposit Account Interest (amount received)	£1,600

Brian had £2,320 deducted during 2014/15 under PAYE. He is entitled to a personal allowance of £10,000.

Required:

Prepare Brian's Income Tax Computation for the tax year, including calculations of his total income tax liability, and the part of this amount that has yet to be paid.

3.5 Major Player had part-time employment income of £5,000 (gross) in 2014/15, on which he paid no tax under PAYE. He has provided you with the following details of the amounts that he has received from his investments. He is entitled to a personal allowance of £10,000.

Date Received	Details	Amount Rec'd
		£
31/3/2014	Osborne Bank Deposit Account Interest	190.00
31/5/2014	Dividend from Growth plc	3,600.00
30/6/2014	3.5% War Loan Interest ('Gilt')	1,500.00
30/9/2014	Interest from Nationside cash NISA	300.00
31/1/2015	Bank of Northumberland Deposit A/C Interest	9,500.00
31/3/2015	Osborne Bank Deposit Account Interest	600.00
30/6/2015	Dividend from Growth plc	1,600.00

Required:

(a) Produce schedules of the amounts of savings and dividend income assessable in the tax year, and the amounts of tax deducted at source and tax credits.

(b) Prepare an Income Tax Computation for the tax year, including calculations of his total income tax liability, and the part of this amount that has yet to be paid, or refunded.

3.6 Some taxable interest is received gross, and some is received net of 20% tax. Examine the following list of income sources, and analyse it into the way that interest is received, using the table.

Bank accounts

Government Securities (Gilts)

Building society accounts

Loan stock from unquoted companies

Received net	Received gross

3.7 New individual savings accounts (NISAs) are subject to various rules. Select from the following, the rules that apply from 1 July 2014.

	✔
Cash NISAs and stocks and shares NISAs are subject to a maximum total investment in the tax year of £15,000	
Investment can be made in cash NISAs during the tax year with any number of providers	
Joint NISA accounts can be opened, but only by married couples	
NISAs can only be opened by individuals who are resident in the UK	
At the end of the tax year the tax-free status of investments made in a stocks and shares NISA expires	
The total invested in a stocks and shares NISA can subsequently be transferred to a cash NISA	

4 Income from employment

this chapter covers...

In this chapter we look in detail at one of the most important categories of personal tax – employment income.

We start by explaining the basis of assessment, and then discuss the difference between employment and being self-employed.

A major section in this chapter relates to benefits in kind. These are non-cash rewards for employees and the rules for calculating the assessable amounts are rather complicated. We will examine the rules that apply to company cars and their fuel, cheap loans, living accommodation and the provision of various other assets and benefits. We will also list benefits that are exempt from any tax charge.

We then move on to a section about expenses. These are payments that an employee makes in connection with his employment that may be reimbursed by his employer. We will examine the rules about when such expenses can be treated as an allowable deduction in the calculation of assessable employment income.

Next we will see how the employment supplementary pages of the tax return are completed. The chapter is completed by a short section on record keeping.

THE BASIS OF ASSESSMENT FOR EMPLOYMENT INCOME

Income from employment is assessed under 'Employment, Pensions and Social Security Income', and the income tax is normally collected through Pay-As-You-Earn (PAYE). We will generally include this in the income tax computation simply as 'employment income'. The basis of assessment is:

	gross income **received** in the tax year
plus	the assessable value of any benefits in kind,
less	any allowable deductions
equals	assessable income from employment

You will notice that (like savings and investment income) we are using a **cash basis** to determine which tax year any receipts are linked to, not an accruals basis. The period in which the income was earned may therefore not always be the one in which it is assessed; this could apply for example to commissions or bonuses that are earned in one period, but paid to the employee in a later one. You should therefore disregard any reference to the period in which employment income was earned, and concentrate just on when it was received. The only exception to this rule is the rare situation when an employee becomes entitled to income but chooses to receive it at a later date. In this case it is taxable in the tax year in which the employee is entitled to the income. As well as income from current employment, this category of income also includes pensions received and certain social security benefits.

employment and self-employment

The income from employment includes salaries, wages, bonuses, commissions, fees and gratuities (tips) where they relate to a job or office. It is important to distinguish between the concept of being employed (and having employment income) and being self-employed, the income from which is assessed as 'trading income'. Employment income results from an employment contract (even an implied one) where the employer exerts control over the employee. A self-employed person or contractor has much more control over the way he or she operates.

The distinction is whether the contract that applies is one **of service** (when the person is an **employee**), or a contract **for services** (a **self-employed** relationship). These can be confusing phrases, but if you think a contract

■ **of service** could apply to a servant (where the employee serves the employer)

■ **for services** could apply to someone who invoices 'for services rendered' and is self employed

In some cases it can be difficult to establish whether the person is employed or self employed, and HMRC have produced leaflets and an online 'Employment Status Indicator' tool to help.

The following are indicators that help provide evidence in one direction or the other.

Indicators of Employment	Indicators of Self Employment
Need to do the work yourself	Can employ helper or substitute
Told how, where and when to do work	Decide yourself how, when and where to do work
Work set hours and paid regular wage with sick pay and holidays	Choose work hours and invoice for work done
No risk of capital or losses	Risk own capital and bear losses from work that is not to standard
Employer provides equipment	Provide own equipment
Work for one employer (but sometimes more)	Work for several people or organisations

BENEFITS IN KIND

You will have noticed that employment income includes the assessable value of '**benefits in kind**'. This is the term used to describe any reward that an employee receives because of his employment that is not paid in money. It can therefore apply to a range of 'non-cash' items ranging from use of a company car to holidays paid for by the employer.

There are some situations where a payment on behalf of an employee may count as a benefit in kind, but the expense incurred would also be considered an **allowable deduction**, thereby cancelling out the effect of any tax charge. We will examine these situations in the 'allowable deductions' section later in this chapter.

Originally, benefits were assessed based on the cash cost to the employer of providing the employee with the benefit. While this rule is still used in some situations, there are now many types of benefit where specific rules are used to calculate the assessable amounts. Through this section we will now look at the more important benefits and how they are assessed. Although this is a complicated area you must learn how to deal with all these examples, as they are popular examination topics.

company cars

A car owned (or leased) by the employer, but available for both business and private use by an employee is an assessable benefit. Most company cars have at least some private use, since the journey to and from work is considered private rather than business mileage. The way that the benefit is calculated is very specific, and is divided into two separate types of benefit:

■ **a scale charge for having private use of the car** – the assessable amount is a percentage of the car's list price, and is deemed to include all the costs of the car, except fuel. It therefore includes road tax, insurance, repairs and servicing etc, and none of these costs are assessable separately

■ **a scale charge for using fuel for private motoring** if this is paid for by the employer

We will describe the two benefits in turn.

scale charges for private use of cars

The scale charge for having use of the car depends on:

■ the list price of the car when new, and
■ the car's carbon dioxide emissions, measured in grams per kilometre (g/km), and
■ whether the car is petrol or diesel

The system works by using percentages linked to emission levels. The appropriate percentage (up to 35%) is then applied to the list price of the car when new, and the result forms the assessable amount of the benefit. The higher the emissions, therefore, the higher the percentage and the higher the taxable benefit. The percentages change from time to time, since it is expected that typical emission levels will generally fall as new models are introduced.

For 2014/15 the charge for petrol or electric cars works as follows:

■ for cars that do not emit any carbon dioxide when driven ('zero' emission cars), there is no charge (i.e. 0%)
■ for cars with emissions of 75g/km or less the charge is 5% of the list price
■ for cars between 76g/km and 94g/km the charge is 11%
■ for cars of 95g/km or more the charge is 12%, rising by 1% for every 5g/km over the 95g/km level, up to a maximum of 35%

So, for example, cars with emissions of 105g/km would have a charge of 14% of list price, and cars with emissions of 110g/km would have a charge of 15%.

Before calculating the percentage, the car's emission level (if above 95) is rounded down to a multiple of 5 (eg 199 would be rounded down to 195).

example

If an employee is provided with a petrol engine car with a list price of £20,000, and an emission level of 203 g/km throughout 2014/15, then the assessable benefit would be calculated as:

Percentage: $12\% + (1\% \times (200 - 95) / 5)$

                 $= 12\% + 21\%$ $= 33\%$.

The 33% is then multiplied by the list price of the car:

Benefit: $£20,000 \times 33\% = £6,600$.

The percentages that apply to diesel cars are 3% more than those for petrol powered cars. This is because diesel cars naturally have slightly lower emission levels than similar petrol models. The lowest percentage charge for a diesel car is therefore $5\% + 3\% = 8\%$.

Both petrol and diesel cars are subject to a maximum percentage of 35%.

example

If an employee is provided with a diesel engine car with a list price of £15,000, and an emission level of 172 grams per kilometre throughout 2014/15, then the assessable benefit would be:

$£15,000 \times (12\% + 15\% + 3\% = 30\%) = £4,500$.

You will need to remember how to carry out the calculations for petrol and diesel cars.

The exempt benefit that applies to 'zero emission' cars could apply (for example) to cars powered solely by electricity. Hybrid cars with a conventional engine plus an electric engine will have an emission level and the calculation will be carried out as normal.

The figure calculated is adjusted in the following circumstances:

■ where the car is not available to the employee for the whole tax year, the assessable amount is time-apportioned – this is a common adjustment in examination tasks. Note that for a period of time to count when the car is 'unavailable' it must be a continuous period of 30 days or more. So, for example, if a car could not be used because it was being repaired for 25 days then there would be no time-apportionment

■ where the employee makes a **revenue** contribution to the employer for the use of the car, this is deducted from the assessable amount that would otherwise apply

■ where the employee makes a **capital** contribution towards the cost of the car, this contribution, up to a maximum of £5,000, is deducted from the list price before the appropriate percentage is applied

- where accessories or modifications are added to the car before or at the time that the car is first made available to the employee their cost is added to the list price. This would not apply however to equipment to enable a disabled person to use the car, nor to equipment which is necessary for the use of the car in the performance of the employee's duties (for example a tow bar if the employee was required to tow a trailer for his job). There is also an exception for the provision of special security equipment (e.g. bullet resistant glass) where it is necessary due to the employee's role

- where accessories are added to the car later on these are added to the list price and applied to the whole tax year in which they were added. This only applies however to accessories that cost more than £100 each (or per set)

- where the company car is a 'classic' car over 15 years old at the end of the tax year and has a market value which is both over £15,000 and exceeds the list price, then the market value is used instead of the list price

- where an employee is provided with a chauffeur in addition to a company car, the cost of the chauffeur forms an additional assessable benefit

example

An employee was provided with a petrol engine company car for the whole of 2014/15. The list price of the car was £25,000, and emissions were 123g/km. The employee made a capital contribution towards the cost of the car of £7,000. In September 2014 the company paid for a set of 4 alloy wheels for the car. They cost £95 each.

The list price would be increased by the cost of the set of alloy wheels of £380 (applicable for the whole tax year), and there would be a deduction from the list price relating to the employee's capital contribution, but this would be limited to £5,000. The assessable benefit would therefore be:

£20,380 x (12% + 5% = 17%) = £3,464 (rounded down)

fuel benefit for private use of company cars

When an employee is provided with a company car, the employer may agree to pay for the fuel that the employee uses for private mileage as well as for business use. If this happens, a further assessable benefit arises, calculated as follows:

In **2014/15** the same percentage as is applied to the car (based on its emissions), is multiplied by a fixed amount of £21,700.

---

example

If an employee is provided with a petrol engine car with a list price of £20,000, and an emission level of 203 g/km throughout 2014/15, then the assessable **fuel benefit** would be:

£21,700 x 33% = £7,161 (by applying the emission percentage to the fixed amount of £21,700).

The fuel charge is time-apportioned if the car, for which private fuel is provided, is not available for the whole tax year. The same rule regarding a car being unavailable for at least 30 days applies to fuel as well as use of the car. Note however that the same fuel charge applies if the employee has **any** fuel provided for private mileage, no matter how little or how much. Unlike the car benefit itself, making a contribution to the employer will have no effect on the assessable benefit for fuel. The only way for an employee to avoid the charge is to pay privately (or reimburse the employer) for **all** private fuel that has been used.

pool cars

Pool cars are cars whose use is shared amongst employees for business purposes. There is no assessable benefit for employees who use pool cars, but the definition of a pool car is strict. To qualify as a non-assessable pool car it must:

- be primarily used for business purposes and any private use must be incidental
- be used by several employees, and
- not normally be kept at an employee's home

vans

Where an employer provides a small van that can be used privately there is a scale charge. The assessable benefit for 2014/15 is £3,090. This amount does not include any private fuel, which is assessed separately – currently based on an amount of £581 per year. Where the employee uses the van privately only for travel between home and work and insignificant other private use, this will not be classed as a benefit.

If a van is 'zero emission' (for example powered solely by electricity) then there is no assessable benefit for private use.

cheap (or 'beneficial') loans

Where a loan is granted to an employee and charged at less than the HM Revenue & Customs official interest rate, there may be an assessable benefit. This official rate was 3.25% pa at the time that this book was published. This rate does change from time to time. You will be provided with the current official rate in an examination, which must be used to gain maximum marks.

The benefit is calculated as the difference between the interest charge that would be generated by using the official rate, and the actual interest charged. However, there is no assessable benefit if the loan (or total loans) outstanding is £10,000 or less throughout the tax year 2014/15.

There is also no assessable benefit for a loan (of any amount) that is used entirely to purchase equipment (but not cars etc) for wholly business use.

If a loan (of any amount) is written-off by the employer then the whole amount is assessable.

example

An employer provides his employee with a £15,000 loan at an interest rate of 2% per year.

The actual interest charge would be £300 per year, assuming no capital repayments.

The assessable benefit would therefore be (£15,000 x 3.25%) minus £300 = £187 (rounded down).

The above example was based on a simple situation where the same amount was outstanding for the whole tax year. Where examples are more complex, with part repayments being made there are two calculation methods which HMRC will accept:

■ the first method is to calculate **exactly** the interest figures based on the balances owed for each proportion of the year

■ the second is a simple **average** method which we will explain below. This is the method that you will be expected to use in your examination where necessary

The following method is used to work out the assessable benefit of a single loan. If there were more than one loan the method would be applied to each loan and the final results added together.

■ start with the loan balance at either the start of the tax year or the start of the loan if later

■ add the loan balance at either the end of the tax year or just before the loan ended if earlier

■ divide the total of these figures by 2

■ time apportion this based on complete months of the loan (e.g. 6/12 for a loan that was only held for 6 months in the tax year)

■ multiply this by the difference between the official interest rate (currently 3.25%) and the rate paid (if any)

example

John was granted a loan from his employer of £15,000 on 1 January 2014 at an interest rate of 2%. John repaid £4,000 on 1 July 2014, and then repaid the remaining £11,000 on 6 January 2015.

Balance at start of tax year 2014/15 (since the loan was taken out before this)	£15,000
Balance just before repayment (since this occurred before the end of the tax year)	£11,000
	£26,000
	÷ 2 = £13,000

£13,000 x 9/12 (months of loan in this tax year) x (3.25% – 2%) = £121 (rounded down)

The assessable amount will be £121

Note that in this example the date of the partial repayment was not relevant.

living accommodation

Where the employer provides free accommodation for an employee, this can result in an assessable benefit. Unless an exemption applies (as we will see later in this section), the assessable benefit works as follows:

- the assessable amount for the accommodation itself is normally the **higher** of the 'annual value' (based on the rateable value), and the rent paid by the employer (if the property is not owned by the employer)

- where the accommodation was purchased by the employer, and cost more than £75,000 then an additional assessment is applied. This is based on the excess of the purchase price over £75,000 multiplied by the HM Revenue & Customs official interest rate. This is the same rate (currently 3.25%) that is used to calculate the benefit of cheap loans as described above

- the cost figure is increased by any capital expenditure incurred on the property between the date of purchase and the start of the current tax year. Any capital expenditure during the current tax year is therefore ignored for this year's calculation, but will be used in the following tax year

- the cost of any other living expenses paid by the employer would be added to the assessment (for example electricity costs). Furniture and other assets provided by the employer will also result in an assessable benefit as we will see in the next section

- if an employee does not have use of the accommodation for the whole tax year, then any assessable benefit (as described above) would be time-apportioned

- any rent or similar amount paid by the employee to the employer for use of the accommodation is deducted from the benefit figure calculated

example

An employee is allowed to live in a company flat free of charge throughout the tax year. The annual value of the flat is £1,500, and the employer also pays the heating costs of the flat which amount to £600 per year.

The flat cost the employer £100,000 when it was originally purchased.

Assuming that the employee could not claim any exemption from the flat being assessable, the amount would be calculated as follows:

Annual value	£1,500
Additional charge (£100,000 – £75,000) x 3.25%	£812
Other expenses paid by employer	£600
Total assessable benefit	£2,912

If the accommodation was only available to the employee for 6 months of the tax year the benefit would be £2,912 x 6/12 = £1,456.

For the accommodation itself to result in no assessable benefit one of the following situations must apply:

■ the employee is a representative occupier (for example a caretaker)

■ it is customary to provide the employee with accommodation in that particular job (for example a vicar)

■ the accommodation is provided for security reasons

These situations are sometimes referred to as 'job related accommodation'.

Note that in these situations the annual value and additional charge for properties over £75,000 is not applied. However any running expenses of the accommodation (except council tax and water charges) that are paid for by the employer will still result in an assessable benefit. In these circumstances the benefit of such costs will be restricted to a maximum of 10% of the employee's earnings from the job.

provision of other assets

Where an asset is given to an employee then the assessable benefit is the market value of the asset at that time. Apart from vehicles, if an asset is provided for an employee's private use (but remains belonging to the employer) then there is an assessable benefit of 20% of the market value of the asset when first provided.

If the asset that the employee has private use of is rented or hired by the employer (instead of owned) then the assessable benefit is the **higher** of:

■ 20% of the market value when first provided, and

■ the rental or hire charge paid by the employer

This benefit would apply to each tax year that it was used by the employee.

If an asset that was provided in this way is subsequently given to the employee (or he/she buys it from the employer) then a further benefit may arise based on the higher of:

- market value at the date of the transfer, and
- market value when first provided, less benefits for use of the asset already assessed

From the higher of these figures is deducted any amount paid by the employee.

example

An employee is provided with the use of a home entertainment system, when its market value was £1,000. Two years later he buys it from the employer, paying £100, when its market value was £300.

The benefit assessed for each year that it was owned by the employer and the employee used it would be £1,000 x 20% = £200.

The benefit assessed upon purchase would be the higher of:

- market value at the date of the transfer, (£300), and
- market value when first provided, less benefits assessed already (£1,000 – £200 – £200 = £600)

ie £600, minus amount paid by the employee of £100 = £500.

These calculations would also apply to furniture owned by the employer in accommodation used by an employee.

vouchers, credit cards, and other benefits paid by the employer

Where an employee is provided with a voucher that can be spent in a specified way, the benefit is the cost to the employer of providing the voucher. This may be less than the face value of the voucher.

For example, suppose an employer gave his employee a £500 voucher at Christmas to spend in a particular store. If the voucher cost the employer £470 then this amount would be the assessable benefit.

If an employee has use of a company credit card then any expenditure will be assessable, except:

- business expenditure that qualifies as an allowable deduction (see next section), and
- expenditure on benefits that are assessed separately (for example in connection with a company car or its fuel)

Where an employer provides an employee with goods or services for private use, the cost to the employer is the assessable amount. This could arise if an employer paid for a holiday for an employee, or paid their train fare from home to work.

tax-free benefits

The following is a summary of the main benefits that are not taxable i.e. that are excluded from the benefits included in assessable employment income. Some of these have already been mentioned earlier in this chapter:

- private use of a 'zero emission' car or van

- use of a van provided by the employer, provided the only non-business use is travel from home to work and other insignificant private mileage

- private use of a bicycle and helmet provided by the employer if used to commute to work

- travel on employer's buses which are used mainly for qualifying journeys

- disabled people's cost of travel between home and work

- the following employer-supported childcare:
    - childcare provided by the employer, for example, a workplace creche
    - provision of childcare vouchers up to £55 per week that can be used to pay for approved childcare
    - payment directly to an approved child carer up to £55 per week for childcare

  These limits of £55 per week apply to basic rate taxpayers and are reduced to £28 per week for higher rate taxpayers and £25 per week for additional rate taxpayers who begin to receive this benefit after 5 April 2011.

  Note that this tax exemption does not apply to cash payments made directly to an employee.

- an allowance to cover incidental expenses while working away from home of up to £5 per night while in the UK and £10 per night while overseas

- overseas medical treatment or medical insurance while working abroad

- workplace parking

- a loan from the employer at a low, or nil rate of interest, providing the loan does not exceed £10,000 at any time during the tax year or is to purchase equipment entirely for business use

- meals at a staff canteen – provided it is available to all staff

- in-house sports facilities (not facilities available to general public)

- counselling services

- up to one health screening assessment and one medical check up in any year

- free eye checks for employees with significant use of computers at work

- employers' contributions to pension schemes

- mobile telephone provided by employer (including cost of calls) – limited to one per employee

- an allowance of £4 per week to cover expenses incurred by employees required by their employer to work at home
- provision of a late night taxi to take an employee home after irregular working later than usual until at least 9pm (fewer than 60 times a year)
- goodwill entertainment for an employee that is provided by someone other than the employer (and not connected with the employer)
- goodwill gifts for an employee (goods or voucher for goods) that is provided by someone other than the employer (and not connected with the employer), restricted to a cost of £250 or less
- payment of a qualifying award under a staff suggestion scheme – up to a maximum of £5,000
- long service awards to employees with 20 years or more service (and there has been no similar award in the previous 10 years), based on a value of up to £50 per year of service; the award can be in the form of shares or a tangible asset
- relocation costs of up to £8,000 on a change of residence due to a change in the place of work
- retraining costs to help to get another job
- costs of work-related training for practical or theoretical skills that you are reasonably likely to need in current or future jobs with your employer
- costs of annual staff parties which are open to staff generally and cost no more than £150 per head
- scholarships to employees' children from a trust fund or scheme open to the public under which not more than 25% of the total payments relate to employees (otherwise these are taxable)
- air miles or points to obtain gifts when obtained by employees in the same way as members of the public (even if for business expenditure)
- damages or compensation which is employment related
- reimbursement of expenses that are incurred on behalf of the employer, or that are an allowable deduction – see next section

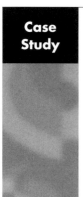

Case Study

BENNY FITT: EMPLOYMENT INCOME INCLUDING BENEFITS IN KIND

Benny Fitt works as a Sales Manager for ESP Limited. He was employed throughout 2014/15 at a basic salary of £25,000 per year, plus a six-monthly bonus dependent on his performance. He received the following bonus payments:

Period related to bonus	Amount	Date Received
July - Dec 2013	£2,000	28/2/14
Jan - June 2014	£2,400	31/8/14
July - Dec 2014	£2,700	28/2/15
Jan - June 2015	£3,000	31/8/15

He was provided with a diesel engine car with a list price of £25,000 and an emission rating of 192 g/km from the beginning of the tax year until 5 December.

After that date the car was exchanged for a petrol engine car with a list price of £15,000 and an emission rating of 119 g/km, which was kept until after the end of the tax year. Benny was provided with free fuel for private purposes for both cars.

He was granted an interest-free loan of £12,000 by ESP Limited on 6/4/14. He had not made any repayments by 5/4/15.

Benny was also provided with a home cinema system on 6/4/13 with a value of £800 at that time. On 6/4/14 he bought the system from the company for £250, when its second-hand value was £400.

required

Calculate the assessable amount of employment income for Benny for the tax year 2014/15. Assume that the HM Revenue & Customs official interest rate is 3.25% throughout the year.

solution

salary and bonuses:

The date that the money was received determines which tax year it is assessed in. This gives the following figures for 2014/15:

		£
Basic Salary		25,000
Bonuses –	rec'd 31 August 14	2,400
	rec'd 28 Feb 15	2,700
		30,100

The other bonuses are assessed before or after the year that we are concerned with.

company cars

The assessable benefit of each car is calculated separately, based on the proportion of the tax year that it is provided.

Car one is based on a percentage of (12% + 19% + 3%) = 34%.
The assessable benefit for this car is therefore:

34% x £25,000 x 8/12 =	£5,666

Car two is based on a percentage of 16% (12% + 4%).
The assessable benefit for this car is therefore:

16% x £15,000 x 4/12 =	£800
Total company car benefit	£6,466

car fuel

Car one: 34% x £21,700 x 8/12 =	£4,918
Car two: 16% x £21,700 x 4/12 =	£1,157
Total car fuel benefit	£6,075

interest-free loan

Since the full amount is outstanding throughout the year, and no interest is charged, the benefit is based on the amount lent multiplied by the official rate.

£12,000 x 3.25%	£390

home cinema

In the first year (2013/14) 20% of the value is charged (£160). In the second year (2014/15) the charge is based on the original value less previous benefit, since this is greater than the second-hand value.

(£800 – £160) minus £250 paid by Benny	£390

Employment Income Summary

	£
Salary & Bonuses	30,100
Company Cars	6,466
Car Fuel	6,075
Loan	390
Home Cinema	390
Employment income assessable amount	43,421

ALLOWABLE DEDUCTIONS

We will now examine the amounts that can be deducted from the income and benefits received in respect of employment, and therefore reduce the employment income assessment. These are specific amounts that the employee has paid out in connection with the employment.

The general rule is that to be allowable against employment income, expenditure must be incurred **wholly, exclusively and necessarily** in the performance of the duties of the employment. You may recognise part of this phrase from our studies of property income; but here the word 'necessarily' is added. This means that strictly speaking allowable expenditure must be for something that the employment duties could not be carried out without – not just that the job is carried out more easily or efficiently because of the expenditure. For example, personal clothing is not an allowable deduction, even if it was bought especially for work and only worn to work. There are specific instances where expenditure is allowable outside this stringent test, but you should use this basic rule when you come across expenditure that you are unsure how to treat.

expenditure reimbursed by the employer

When an employee's expenditure is reimbursed (usually through an 'expenses' claim) the following tax implications are possible:

■ where there is a '**dispensation**' in force from HM Revenue & Customs, it means that it is agreed in advance that expenses will only be paid for allowable expenditure. This means that the reimbursement automatically cancels out the original expenditure and there is no effect on tax and no need to enter the details on a tax return

■ if there isn't a dispensation in force, the reimbursement may still be for expenditure that is allowable. This means that the amount received from the employer is treated as a benefit, but the expenditure by the employee is an allowable deduction. If these amounts are identical they will cancel each other out, but they still need to be shown separately on the tax return, as we will see later

We will now look at how to deal with some specific types of expenditure. These items may or may not be reimbursed by an employer.

using your own transport for business

This relates to travelling within the job, (eg journeys from one site to another) not for travelling from home to the normal workplace (which counts as private motoring). HM Revenue & Customs has published mileage rates that constitute allowable expenditure as follows.

Cars and vans:	First 10,000 miles in tax year	45p per mile
	Additional mileage	25p per mile
Motor cycles:		24p per mile
Bicycles:		20p per mile

Note that this does not apply to company cars – only for use of the employees' own transport. It may well be that the employer reimburses a mileage allowance. Where this is exactly in line with these figures the benefit received cancels out the allowable expenditure, but if it is at a higher rate the excess is a net taxable benefit. If the rates paid by the employer are lower (or expenses are not reimbursed at all) then the shortfall is a net allowable deduction. This system is known as 'Approved Mileage Allowance Payments' (AMAP).

entertaining and subsistence

Where an employee incurs expenditure on the costs of spending time away from his/her normal place of work, these costs are normally allowable. Entertaining of the employer's clients is only allowable if the employer has reimbursed the employee, and then the benefit will not be chargeable.

professional fees & subscriptions

Where an employee pays a professional fee or subscription to an organisation that is relevant to his or her employment the cost is an allowable expense. HM Revenue & Customs has a list of approved bodies (available on its website), and the AAT is amongst the accountancy bodies on the list. Where the employer pays the subscription for the employee the benefit received is cancelled out by the allowable deduction.

pension contributions

Contributions that an employee makes to an approved pension scheme are allowable deductions within employment income. If the contributions are made to a scheme run by the employer, then the deduction will often be made automatically before PAYE is operated on the balance of income. If this is the situation, then amounts shown on an employee's P45 and P60 will represent income after the employee's pension contribution has been deducted. You may recall that the employer's contribution to an approved pension scheme is not taxable as a part of an employee's income, so the employee gains two advantages if both he/she and his/her employer contribute to such a scheme. If an employer makes contributions into a pension scheme, but the employee does not contribute, this is known as a 'non-contributory' pension scheme.

payroll giving scheme

Where an arrangement has been made between an employer and an approved Payroll Giving Agency, employees can authorise deductions (without limit) through the payroll of donations to charities. This is allowed as a deduction from earnings, and the employer is able to operate PAYE on the income after the donation has been deducted – just like employees' pension contributions. The employee therefore gets tax relief on his/her donations, and the employer passes the gross amount of the donations onto the Payroll Giving Agency, and this organisation distributes the amounts to the named charities.

Case Study

AL LOWE:
BENEFITS AND ALLOWABLE DEDUCTIONS

Al is employed as an administrator by Spencer & Company, and is paid a gross salary of £22,000 per year. He makes a contribution of 5% of his salary to the company pension scheme, (a scheme that is approved by HM Revenue & Customs). Spencer & Company also pays a contribution into the pension fund of 8% of Al's salary.

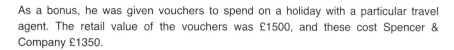

As a bonus, he was given vouchers to spend on a holiday with a particular travel agent. The retail value of the vouchers was £1500, and these cost Spencer & Company £1350.

Al is required to undertake business journeys in his own car, for which the company agreed to reimburse him at a rate of 55p per mile. Al used his car for 7,500 business miles during the tax year, and the company paid him the agreed amounts. He also claimed £300 for subsistence allowances while away on company business, and this was also paid to him. Spencer & Company has a dispensation in force with HM Revenue & Customs regarding payments for subsistence.

Al pays an annual subscription to the Association of Administrative Managers (a professional body, approved by HM Revenue & Customs). This amounted to £140. Spencer & Company did not reimburse him for this.

Al also pays £30 per month to Oxfam under the 'payroll giving scheme' organised by Spencer & Company. This amount is deducted each month from his salary.

required

Calculate the assessable amount of employment income for Al for the tax year.

solution

		£
Gross Salary		22,000
less		
	5% pension contribution	(1,100)
	payroll giving scheme	(360)
Amount used for PAYE purposes		20,540
add benefits:		
	Mileage paid in excess of HMRC approved rate	
	7,500 x (55p − 45p)	750
	Cost of holiday vouchers	1,350
less allowable deduction:		
	Professional fee paid	(140)
Assessable amount		22,500

Note that

• the employer's contribution to the pension scheme is not included as a benefit

• the subsistence allowance is covered by a dispensation, and so does not need to be considered further

REDUNDANCY PAYMENTS

Redundancy payments (compensation for loss of employment) are not strictly emoluments, nor are they benefits in kind. The types of redundancy payments, and the rules regarding whether they are taxable can be very complex. Generally the first £30,000 of a redundancy payment is exempt from income tax.

COMPLETING THE EMPLOYMENT PAGES OF THE TAX RETURN

The tax return supplementary page relating to employment is normally one page (E1), as illustrated on page 4.19. The 2013/14 form is shown here as the 2014/15 form was not available when this book was published. One page needs to be completed for each separate employment carried out during the tax year, with page E2 used for a second employment.

■ The main top section of page E1 requires details of your cash-based income from your employments. You may need to complete the following boxes:
- Box 1 is for the gross pay (be careful that this is the figure after most company pension contributions and any payroll giving donations have been deducted).
- Box 2 is for the amount of tax deducted under PAYE.
- Box 3 relates to any tips or other taxable receipts that are not included in box 1.

■ The second section relates to benefits in kind, and will contain the **assessable amount** under each category. The boxes (9 to 16) are quite clearly headed, but note that:
- Box 9 is for the assessable amount of company cars or vans, and box 10 is for the assessable amount of fuel relating to them.
- Box 12 is for both
  • the assessable benefits arising from credit cards and vouchers, and
  • the amount that any mileage allowance paid to an employee exceeds the approved amount. This relates only to the use of an employee's own vehicle
- Box 16 will contain the amount of expenses received (unless they are the subject of a dispensation). If these relate to allowable expenses then an equivalent amount will also be inserted into boxes 17 to 20 in the expenses section below.

■ Allowable expenses and deductions are entered on the final section of the page in boxes 17 to 20. In addition to other business travel and subsistence expenses, box 17 will also be used for claiming the difference where an employer paid a lower mileage allowance than the approved rates.

It is vital that the data entered on the employment pages reconciles with the employment income computation that will have been completed. With the exception of the tax paid amount in box 2, you should check that the total pay and benefits entered in the boxes on page E1, minus the entries under 'expenses' equal the assessable amount.

HM Revenue & Customs

Employment
Tax year 6 April 2013 to 5 April 2014

Your name

Your Unique Taxpayer Reference (UTR)

Complete an *Employment* page for each employment or directorship

1 Pay from this employment – the total from your P45 or P60 – *before tax was taken off*
£

2 UK tax taken off pay in box 1
£

3 Tips and other payments not on your P60 – *read the Employment notes*
£

4 PAYE tax reference of your employer (on your P45/P60)

5 Your employer's name

6 If you were a company director, put 'X' in the box

7 And, if the company was a close company, put 'X' in the box

8 If you are a part-time teacher in England or Wales and are on the Repayment of Teachers' Loans Scheme for this employment, put 'X' in the box

Benefits from your employment – use your form P11D (or equivalent information)

9 Company cars and vans – *the total 'cash equivalent' amount*
£

10 Fuel for company cars and vans – *the total 'cash equivalent' amount*
£

11 Private medical and dental insurance – *the total 'cash equivalent' amount*
£

12 Vouchers, credit cards and excess mileage allowance
£

13 Goods and other assets provided by your employer – *the total value or amount*
£

14 Accommodation provided by your employer – *the total value or amount*
£

15 Other benefits (including interest-free and low interest loans) – *the total 'cash equivalent' amount*
£

16 Expenses payments received and balancing charges
£

Employment expenses

17 Business travel and subsistence expenses
£

18 Fixed deductions for expenses
£

19 Professional fees and subscriptions
£

20 Other expenses and capital allowances
£

ℹ Share schemes, employment lump sums, compensation, deductions and Seafarers' Earnings Deduction are on the *Additional information* pages enclosed in the tax return pack.

SA102 2014   Page E 1   HMRC 12/13

We will now demonstrate how to complete the employment page by using the data from the two Case Studies that were used earlier in this chapter.

Case Study

BENNY FITT:
COMPLETING THE TAX RETURN EMPLOYMENT PAGE

Benny Fitt works as a Sales Manager for ESP Limited. His assessable amount of employment income for 2014/15 has already been calculated (see pages 4.12 - 4.14), and is summarised as follows.

Employment Income Summary

	£
Salary & Bonuses	30,100
Company Cars	6,466
Car Fuel	6,075
Loan	390
Home Cinema	390
Assessable amount	43,421

required

Complete the relevant employment page for Benny for 2014/15.

solution

The completed form (using the 2013/14 version) is shown opposite. We have not been given full employment details or a figure for income tax deducted in this case, so boxes 2 and 4 have been left blank.

Most of the entries are self-explanatory, but note that the transfer of the home cinema is shown in box 13. If the form related to the previous year, when Benny just had use of the home cinema then the benefit would also be shown in box 13.

Check to make sure that you can follow how the form has been completed, so that you could complete a similar exercise if required.

HM Revenue & Customs

Employment
Tax year 6 April 2013 to 5 April 2014

Your name

B E N N Y   F I T T

Your Unique Taxpayer Reference (UTR)

Complete an *Employment* page for each employment or directorship

1. **Pay from this employment – the total from your P45 or P60** - *before tax was taken off*

   £ 3 0 1 0 0 · 0 0

2. **UK tax taken off pay in box 1**

   £ · 0 0

3. **Tips and other payments not on your P60** - *read the Employment notes*

   £ · 0 0

4. **PAYE tax reference of your employer (on your P45/P60)**

   /

5. **Your employer's name**

   E S P   L I M I T E D

6. **If you were a company director, put 'X' in the box**

7. **And, if the company was a close company, put 'X' in the box**

8. **If you are a part-time teacher in England or Wales and are on the Repayment of Teachers' Loans Scheme for this employment, put 'X' in the box**

Benefits from your employment - use your form P11D (or equivalent information)

9. **Company cars and vans** - *the total 'cash equivalent' amount*

   £ 6 4 6 6 · 0 0

10. **Fuel for company cars and vans** - *the total 'cash equivalent' amount*

    £ 6 0 7 5 · 0 0

11. **Private medical and dental insurance** - *the total 'cash equivalent' amount*

    £ · 0 0

12. **Vouchers, credit cards and excess mileage allowance**

    £ · 0 0

13. **Goods and other assets provided by your employer** - *the total value or amount*

    £ 3 9 0 · 0 0

14. **Accommodation provided by your employer** - *the total value or amount*

    £ · 0 0

15. **Other benefits (including interest-free and low interest loans)** - *the total 'cash equivalent' amount*

    £ 3 9 0 · 0 0

16. **Expenses payments received and balancing charges**

    £ · 0 0

Employment expenses

17. **Business travel and subsistence expenses**

    £ · 0 0

18. **Fixed deductions for expenses**

    £ · 0 0

19. **Professional fees and subscriptions**

    £ · 0 0

20. **Other expenses and capital allowances**

    £ · 0 0

ⓘ **Share schemes, employment lump sums, compensation, deductions and Seafarers' Earnings Deduction** are on the *Additional information* pages enclosed in the tax return pack.

AL LOWE:
COMPLETING THE TAX RETURN EMPLOYMENT PAGE

Al Lowe is an administrator, employed by Spencer & Company. His employment income computation for 2014/15 has already been produced from information provided and is summarised below:

Gross Salary	22,000
less	
5% pension contribution	(1,100)
payroll giving scheme	(360)
Amount used for PAYE purposes	20,540
add benefits:	
Mileage paid in excess of HMRC approved rate	
7,500 x (55p – 45p)	750
Cost of holiday vouchers	1,350
less allowable deduction:	
Professional fee paid	(140)
Assessable amount	22,500

required

Complete the employment page of the tax return.

solution

The completed form (based on the 2013/14 version) is shown on the next page. You should note the following:

- the amount shown in box 1 is after deducting pension contributions and donations under the 'payroll giving scheme'

- the excess only of the mileage payments is shown in box 12, together with the holiday vouchers

- the professional fees paid are claimed in box 19. If his employer had paid these for him they would also need to be entered in box 16

- the subsistence payments have not been entered on the form, as there is a dispensation in force. If this were not the case they would normally be shown in both boxes 16 and 20 to cancel out their effect

HM Revenue & Customs

Employment
Tax year 6 April 2013 to 5 April 2014

Your name

A L   L O W E

Your Unique Taxpayer Reference (UTR)

Complete an *Employment* page for each employment or directorship

1 Pay from this employment – the total from your **P45 or P60** - *before tax was taken off*

£ 2 0 5 4 0 . 0 0

2 UK tax taken off pay in box 1

£ . 0 0

3 Tips and other payments not on your P60
- *read the Employment notes*

£ . 0 0

4 PAYE tax reference of your employer (on your P45/P60)

[   ] / [   ]

5 Your employer's name

S P E N C E R   &   C O M P A N Y

6 If you were a company director, put 'X' in the box

7 And, if the company was a close company, put 'X' in the box

8 If you are a part-time teacher in England or Wales and are on the Repayment of Teachers' Loans Scheme for this employment, put 'X' in the box

Benefits from your employment - use your form P11D (or equivalent information)

9 Company cars and vans
- *the total 'cash equivalent' amount*

£ . 0 0

10 Fuel for company cars and vans
- *the total 'cash equivalent' amount*

£ . 0 0

11 Private medical and dental insurance
- *the total 'cash equivalent' amount*

£ . 0 0

12 Vouchers, credit cards and excess mileage allowance

£ 2 1 0 0 . 0 0

13 Goods and other assets provided by your employer
- *the total value or amount*

£ . 0 0

14 Accommodation provided by your employer
- *the total value or amount*

£ . 0 0

15 Other benefits (including interest-free and low interest loans) - *the total 'cash equivalent' amount*

£ . 0 0

16 Expenses payments received and balancing charges

£ . 0 0

Employment expenses

17 Business travel and subsistence expenses

£ . 0 0

18 Fixed deductions for expenses

£ . 0 0

19 Professional fees and subscriptions

£ 1 4 0 . 0 0

20 Other expenses and capital allowances

£ . 0 0

KEEPING RECORDS

Employment income records, like those for savings and dividend income, need to be kept for at least a year after the online tax return must be submitted. For example, the employment income records for the tax year 2014/15 would need to be kept by the employee until at least 31/1/17.

Typical records that an employee should keep to substantiate his or her tax position include:

■ P60 form(s) that summarise income and tax from the employment(s)

■ P11D form(s) that give details of benefits and expenses of the employment(s) (where applicable)

■ receipts or invoices to substantiate payments made that count as allowable deductions

■ a copy of the employment pages of the tax return

Chapter Summary

■ Income from employment is categorised as 'Income from Employment, Pensions and Social Security'. The basis of assessment is the gross income received in the tax year, plus the assessable value of any benefits in kind, less any allowable deductions. Employers are required to operate the PAYE system whereby tax is deducted from payments made to employees throughout the tax year.

■ Benefits in kind are generally assessed on the cost to the employer of providing the benefit. However many more specific rules have been developed to calculate the assessable amount of certain benefits.

■ Company cars that are available for an employee's private use have an assessable amount based on a percentage of the list price of the car. The percentage will depend on the carbon dioxide emission rating of the car, and whether it has an electric, petrol or diesel engine. Fuel for private motoring is assessed using the same percentage that applies to the car, but multiplied by a fixed amount. Pool cars are not assessable, but the conditions to qualify are stringent.

■ Cheap or interest free loans of over £10,000 are assessable on the difference between the 'official' interest rate and the interest charged. Living accommodation may be non-assessable, but otherwise is based on the annual value of the property, plus a supplementary charge for 'expensive' properties owned by the employer. Other assets provided for employees' private use are generally charged at 20% of their value. There are also some specific tax-free benefits.

■ Allowable deductions are generally expenditure that is incurred wholly, exclusively and necessarily in the performance of the duties of the employment. There are also examples of certain expenditure that is allowable, including mileage payments at specified rates, professional fees and subscriptions, and pension contributions. Employees can also make tax-free donations to charities via a 'payroll giving scheme' operated by their employer.

■ Employees who need to complete a tax return must fill in the supplementary page E1. Records must be kept for one year after the latest date for filing the online return.

Key Terms		
	Pay As You Earn (PAYE)	the system that employers must operate whereby income tax is deducted at source from payments made to employees
	benefits in kind	any reward from employment that an employee receives that is not in the form of money
	company car	a car owned (or leased) by the employer that is normally available for both business and private use by an employee
	pool car	a non-assessable car that is available for primarily business use by a range of employees, and is not kept at any employee's home
	beneficial loan	a loan that is at a low interest rate, or is interest free, granted to an employee by an employer
	allowable deductions	expenditure that the employee has incurred that can be deducted in the calculation of the employment income assessable amount
	dispensation	an agreement between HM Revenue & Customs and an employer that certain expenses payments will only be made if they are for costs that form allowable deductions; where a dispensation is in force, the expenditure covered does not need to be entered on an employee's tax return
	payroll giving scheme	a scheme whereby employees can make tax-free donations to charity through their employer's payroll system

Activities

4.1 James is employed as a salesman. He receives a basic salary of £18,000 per year, plus commission that is paid on a quarterly basis in arrears.

During the period 1/1/2014 to 30/6/2015 he earned the following commissions, and received the amounts on the dates shown.

Period Commission Earned	Amount	Date Received
Jan - March 2014	£1,200	30/4/14
April - June 2014	£1,450	31/7/14
July - Sept 2014	£1,080	31/10/14
Oct - Dec 2014	£1,250	31/1/15
Jan - March 2015	£1,390	30/4/15
April - June 2015	£1,710	31/7/15

Required:

Calculate the assessable amount of employment income for 2014/15.

4.2 Analyse the following list of benefits in kind into those that are assessable, and those that are tax-free.

(a) Free meals in a staff canteen available to all staff

(b) Use of a company car (including private use)

(c) Free use of a company flat by the company accountant

(d) A £16,000 loan provided by the employer at 8% p.a. interest

(e) Free UK health insurance

(f) A £2,000 computer available to take home and use privately

(g) Mileage payments at a rate of 40p per mile for using own car to drive from home to a permanent workplace

(h) Use of a 'zero emission' car for business and private use

4.3 Julie Payd works as an Accounting Technician for IOU Limited. She was employed throughout the year at a basic salary of £20,000 per year, plus various benefits as follows:

She was provided with a company car and free private fuel throughout the tax year. The car had a petrol engine with an emission rating of 120 grams per km, and a list price of £11,500.

She had use of a company credit card to pay for fuel for the car. The amounts charged to the card for fuel amounted to £1,100 during the year. At Christmas she also spent £100 on private goods through the credit card with her employer's agreement.

She had her private healthcare insurance premium of £730 paid by IOU Ltd.

Required:

Calculate the assessable amount of employment income for Julie for the tax year.

4.4 Sue Mee is employed as a solicitor by Contrax & Company, and is paid a gross salary of £28,000 per year. She makes a contribution of 6% of her salary to an approved company pension scheme. Contrax & Company also pays a contribution into the pension fund of 7% of Sue's salary.

As a bonus, she was given vouchers to spend in a particular department store. The retail value of the vouchers was £1,000, and these cost Contrax & Company £850.

Sue is required to undertake business journeys in her own car, for which the company agreed to reimburse her at a rate of 60p per mile. She used her car for 11,500 business miles, and the company paid her the agreed amounts.

Sue pays an annual subscription to the Association of Executive Solicitors (a professional body, approved by HM Revenue & Customs). This amounted to £170. Contrax & Company did not reimburse her for this.

Sue was reimbursed £250 for hotel accommodation that she had paid for while on business trips. This was agreed as necessary business expenditure.

Required:

1   Calculate the employment income for Sue for the tax year.

2   Complete page E1 of Sue's tax return (2013/14 version shown on the next page).

HM Revenue & Customs

Employment
Tax year 6 April 2013 to 5 April 2014

Your name

Your Unique Taxpayer Reference (UTR)

Complete an *Employment* page for each employment or directorship

1 Pay from this employment – the total from your
P45 or P60 - *before tax was taken off*

£ · 0 0

2 UK tax taken off pay in box 1

£ · 0 0

3 Tips and other payments not on your P60
- *read the Employment notes*

£ · 0 0

4 PAYE tax reference of your employer (on your P45/P60)

/

5 Your employer's name

6 If you were a company director, put 'X' in the box

7 And, if the company was a close company, put 'X'
in the box

8 If you are a part-time teacher in England or Wales and
are on the Repayment of Teachers' Loans Scheme for
this employment, put 'X' in the box

Benefits from your employment - use your form P11D (or equivalent information)

9 Company cars and vans
- *the total 'cash equivalent' amount*

£ · 0 0

10 Fuel for company cars and vans
- *the total 'cash equivalent' amount*

£ · 0 0

11 Private medical and dental insurance
- *the total 'cash equivalent' amount*

£ · 0 0

12 Vouchers, credit cards and excess mileage allowance

£ · 0 0

13 Goods and other assets provided by your employer
- *the total value or amount*

£ · 0 0

14 Accommodation provided by your employer
- *the total value or amount*

£ · 0 0

15 Other benefits (including interest-free and low
interest loans) - *the total 'cash equivalent' amount*

£ · 0 0

16 Expenses payments received and balancing charges

£ · 0 0

Employment expenses

17 Business travel and subsistence expenses

£ · 0 0

18 Fixed deductions for expenses

£ · 0 0

19 Professional fees and subscriptions

£ · 0 0

20 Other expenses and capital allowances

£ · 0 0

ⓘ Share schemes, employment lump sums, compensation, deductions and Seafarers' Earnings Deduction are on the
Additional information pages enclosed in the tax return pack.

4.5   Lettie Housego was employed by Fease & Company as an estate agent throughout the tax year. She was paid a salary of £20,000 p.a., and contributed 5% of this to the approved company pension scheme. She paid tax through PAYE of £3,350 during the tax year, although she suspects that the tax code used was incorrect.

Lettie was provided with a company car with a list price of £18,000 from the start of the tax year until 5 September. This car had a petrol engine and emission level of 187 g/km. She was not entitled to any private fuel for this car, but Fease & Company paid for business fuel.

From 6 September her car was exchanged for a diesel car with a list price of £20,000 and emissions of 127 g/km. Lettie made a one-off capital contribution towards the cost of this car of £1,000. For this car Fease & Company paid for both business and private fuel.

The company pays for private dental treatment for Lettie. This cost £500.

Lettie had bought her own house through a mortgage arranged by Fease & Company. The £60,000 mortgage is on an interest only basis at a rate of 6.5% p.a.

Lettie also had dividend income of £1,800 (the amount received), and net interest of £1,200 from a savings account with NatEast Bank.

Required:

1   Calculate the assessable amount of employment income for Lettie for the tax year.

2   Calculate the assessable amounts of savings and dividend income for the tax year, and the amount of tax that has effectively been paid on this income.

3   Using an income tax computation for the tax year, calculate the amount of income tax for the year that is still owed by Lettie, or due to her.

4.6   For each statement, tick either employment or self-employment:

	Employment	Self Employment
Contract of service is for:	☐	☐
Contract for services is for:	☐	☐
Choose work hours and charge for work done	☐	☐
No need to provide own equipment	☐	☐
Told how, when and where to do work	☐	☐
Can employ helper or substitute	☐	☐
Correct substandard work at own cost	☐	☐

4.7   **(1)**   On 6 September 2014, Kathy was provided with a company loan of £24,000 on which she pays interest at 3% per annum. The official rate of interest is 3.25%. On 6 January 2015 Kathy repaid £4,000.

What is the benefit in kind for 2014/15?

(2)   When accommodation is purchased by an employer, what is the value of the property above which an additional benefit is applied?

	✔
(a) £50,000	
(b) £70,000	
(c) £75,000	
(d) £100,000	

continued

(3) Would the following accommodation be treated as being job-related?

		Yes	No
(a)	Flat provided for a school caretaker	☐	☐
(b)	Accommodation provided for security reasons	☐	☐
(c)	Accommodation provided for all directors	☐	☐

(4) Edward was provided with accommodation in the form of a flat that the employer rents. It is not job related. The flat has an annual value £6,800 and the employer pays a rent of £550 per month. Edward pays £100 per month towards the private use of the flat. His taxable benefit for the tax year is:

		✔
(a)	£5,600	
(b)	£6,800	
(c)	£6,600	
(d)	£5,400	

(5) Which two of the following statements are correct?

(a) Furniture provided by an employer is taxed at 20% per annum of the market value when first provided.

(b) Furniture provided by an employer is taxed on the cost to the employer in the year of purchase.

(c) Employee's private expenses that are paid by the employer are taxed at 20% per annum of the cost.

(d) Employee's private expenses that are paid by the employer are taxed on the cost to the employer.

for your notes

5 Preparing income tax computations

this chapter covers...

In this chapter we review the issues already covered in this book, and bring them together to ensure that we can carry out comprehensive tax computations.

We will also examine several issues that we have not covered earlier. The first of these is the payment of gift aid to charities. These payments are made net of basic rate tax, and for higher rate taxpayers there is a further adjustment needed in the tax computation.

A similar system operates for payments to personal pension schemes, and we will also illustrate how these work.

Next we will examine the personal allowances that apply to those born before 6 April 1948. This can be a slightly complicated area, since income limits and calculations apply.

We will then examine the tax situation for those individuals with income of £100,000 or more. This can involve a reduced (or eliminated) personal allowance as well as the 'additional' tax band for taxable income over £150,000.

The chapter finishes our study of income tax with a review of payment dates and a summary of the main penalties that can apply when various rules are not complied with.

A REVIEW OF ASSESSABLE INCOME

what we have covered so far

In **Chapter 1** we took an overview of assessable income, and looked in outline at how the income tax computation works. We saw that assessable income is divided into categories so that distinct rules can be applied to each source of income.

The analysis of income that we need to be familiar with is repeated here:

'Property Income'	Rental income from land and property.
'Trading Income'	Profits from trades and professions (the self-employed and those in partnership).
'Savings and Investment Income'	UK Interest and UK Dividends.
'Employment, Pensions and Social Security Income'	Income from employment. Income tax is deducted from employment income under the system known as Pay As You Earn (PAYE).

In **Chapter 2** we looked at income from land and property, and how it is assessed. We also saw how the assessable amount is calculated.

In **Chapter 3** we examined 'savings and investment income' in the form of savings income and dividend income. Again we saw how the basis of assessment is applied, and also learned that savings income and dividend income use different tax rates to other (general) income. These different rates, and the order in which income must be treated in the computation are vital if tax is to be calculated accurately.

In **Chapter 4** we explained income from employment. This is a complex area, and we saw how benefits in kind are assessed, and what allowable deductions can be made from employment income.

The only category of income from the above list that we have not looked at in detail is 'profits from trades and professions' that is assessed as 'trading income'. We do not need to look in any detail at this type of income in this learning area, since instead it forms a major part of the unit covered by Osborne Books' 'Business Tax' text. We just need to include the assessable amount in an income tax computation where appropriate (see Chapter 1, pages 1.11 - 1.13).

summary of tax rates for different sources of income

Set out below is a summary of what we have covered so far and a reminder of the type of income to decide the tax rate used for each source of income.

Assessable Income	Coverage in this book	Type of Income
Property Income Rental income (less allowable expenses), for the tax year, calculated on an accruals basis.	Chapter 2	general
Trading Income Profits (after deducting allowable expenses) for the accounting year that ends in the tax year.	outline only	general
Savings and Investment Income: • Gross interest received in the tax year.	Chapter 3	savings
• Dividends received in the tax year, plus the related tax credits.		dividend
Employment Income Amounts received in the tax year from employment, plus the assessable value of any benefits, less any allowable deductions.	Chapter 4	general

At this stage it is worth reminding ourselves of the different tax rates for general, savings, and dividend income. These rates all use common bands, but we must work up through the bands starting with general income, followed by savings income, and then dividend income.

	General Income	Savings Income	Dividend Income
Additional Rate	45%	45%	37.5%
Higher Rate	40%	40%	32.5%
Basic Rate	20%	20%	10%
Starting Rate	N/A	10%	N/A

If you feel unsure about how the system works, now would be a good point to look again at Chapter 3, where it is explained in detail.

Later on we will be using the mechanism described there to carry out some comprehensive tax computations. Before we do that there are a few further topics regarding tax computations that we must be able to deal with.

EXPENDITURE THAT REDUCES TOTAL INCOME TAX

When we described property income and employment income we saw that some allowable expenditure can be deducted from the income within the category to arrive at the assessable amount. We are now going to look at two specific types of expenditure that reduce the total amount of income tax. They both use the same mechanism for obtaining the tax saving.

The system used is similar but **opposite to** the way that building society interest is received. You will remember that bank and building society interest (being taxable) is received **after** tax has been taken off. The specific payments that we are now going to look at (being tax allowable) are similarly paid after tax has been taken off. This effectively reduces the cost to the individual making the payment.

gift aid payments

Gift aid is a government scheme that allows taxpayers to donate any amount to a charity and obtain tax relief at the highest rate that they pay.

The system operates by allowing the payer to deduct tax at 20% from the amount of the gift. The charity then claims the tax amount from HM Revenue & Customs.

Suppose, for example, a taxpayer makes a donation of £80 to a charity. The effect is to treat the payment as a gift of £100 and the charity will be able to reclaim the £20 from HM Revenue & Customs. Such donations can be for any amount, and can be either a one-off gift or a regular payment. The taxpayer simply has to make a declaration to the charity that the donation(s) are to be considered as falling under the gift aid rules, and provide their name and address.

The tax treatment of gift aid payments in the individual's tax computation is as follows:

- unless the taxpayer pays tax at the higher rate, nothing needs to be done. The payer obtains tax relief by the deduction from the payment
- where the taxpayer does pay tax at higher rate, then in addition to the 20% tax relief obtained when making the payment, the basic rate band is increased by the **gross** amount of the gift. This gives further tax saving by moving some income from the higher rate into the basic rate

So, for our example of a payment of £80 to a charity (gross equivalent of £100) the taxpayer's basic rate band would be increased in 2014/15 from £31,865 to £31,965. This will result in extra income being taxed at 20%, not 40%. The adjustment of the band enables the taxpayer to save a further (40% – 20% = 20%) tax. In this example the extra tax saving is £20. This makes the effective cost of the donation only £60 (ie the total tax saving will be £20 + £20). If the taxpayer has very high income then he would also benefit from the 'additional' rate band starting point also being increased by the gross equivalent of the gift aid payment. This would give an additional tax saving. We will look at the 45% rate in more detail later in this chapter.

Note that gift aid is a separate scheme from payroll giving that we looked at in Chapter 4, although an individual can make donations through both schemes if desired.

personal pension plan payments

All pension schemes work in the same general way from a tax point of view. Contributions to the schemes are allowed tax relief, but when the pension is drawn, the regular proceeds are treated as taxable.

We saw in Chapter 4 that payments to approved **occupational pension schemes** (organised by the employer) are usually given tax relief by deducting an employee's contributions in the calculation of their assessable employment income.

Personal pension plans (PPPs) may be set up by individuals who are employees or self-employed. The term also includes **stakeholder pensions** that were introduced as a government initiative, and are not dependent on the contributor being an employee or self-employed.

The mechanism for obtaining tax relief for PPPs is different from that used for an occupational pension scheme. Instead it is dealt with in the same way as donations under the gift aid scheme.

Contributions are made as net amounts – after 20% tax relief has been deducted from the gross amount payable. As with gift aid donations, the gross amount can be calculated by multiplying the net amount by 100/80. The basic rate tax band is increased by the gross amount of the taxpayer's contribution, and this enables higher rate taxpayers to obtain further relief. There is no other action to be taken in the tax computation.

Suppose a taxpayer, Tom, wanted to make gross contributions to a personal pension plan of £2,500 per year. He would make payments of £2,500 x 80% = £2,000 to his pension provider, who would reclaim the tax of £500, and invest £2,500 in the pension fund.

If he is a basic rate taxpayer, then that is the end of the matter – he has obtained the right amount of tax relief through making payments net. If he is a higher rate taxpayer then a further tax saving will arise through moving £2,500 of his income into the basic rate band from the higher rate band. This extra saving would amount to £2,500 x (40% – 20%) = £500.

We will now use a Case Study to demonstrate how this mechanism works for these two types of payment – pension contributions and gift aid.

Case Study

DEE D'UCT:
EXPENDITURE THAT SAVES TAX

Dee is self-employed, with assessable profits for 2014/15 of £38,000. She also has rental income, with an agreed income of £15,000.

Dee has various investments, and these provided the following amounts in 2014/15:

	Amount Received	Tax Paid / Credit	Assessable Amount
Interest	£ 8,000	£2,000	£10,000
Dividends	£ 5,400	£600	£6,000

required

1   Using an income tax computation, calculate the total tax liability for the tax year, and the part of this amount that Dee has yet to pay.

   Assume that Dee has made no gift aid or personal pension payments.

2   Now assume that in the tax year Dee made the following payments:
   • regular gift aid payments totalling £800 net (gross equivalent £1,000)
   • personal pension plan payments of £1,280 net (equivalent to £1,600 gross)

   You are to recalculate Dee's income tax computation to take account of these two payments, and explain how the tax relief has been obtained.

solution

Task 1	Income Tax Computation 2014/15	
	£	Tax Paid £
Property Income	15,000	-
Trading Income	38,000	-
Interest rec'd (as above)	10,000	2,000
Dividend income (as above)	6,000	600
Total Income	69,000	2,600
less Personal Allowance	10,000	
Taxable Income	59,000	

Analysis of Taxable Income:

	£
General Income (£15,000 + £38,000 – £10,000)	43,000
Savings Income	10,000
Dividend Income	6,000
	59,000

Income Tax Calculation:

General Income:	£	£
£31,865 x 20%	6,373.00	
£11,135 x 40% (the rest of the £43,000)	4,454.00	
£43,000		10,827.00

Savings Income:		
£10,000 x 40% (all in this band)	4,000.00	
		4,000.00

Dividend Income:		
£6,000 x 32.5% (all in this band)	1,950.00	
		1,950.00
Income Tax Liability		16,777.00
less Paid		2,600.00
Income Tax to Pay		14,177.00

The way the tax is calculated for each category of income by working up through the bands is illustrated by the following chart (a format already seen in Chapter 3):

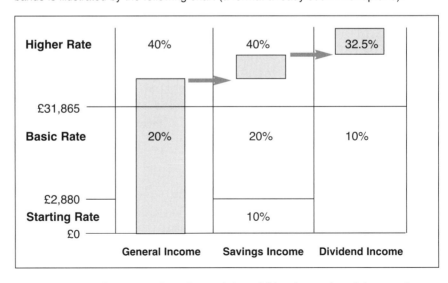

Note that in this diagram we have ignored the additional rate since it is not relevant here.

Task 2

Note firstly that the amounts payable as gift aid (£1,000) and pension plan contributions (£1,600) have only cost Dee £800 + £1,280 = £2,080.

The difference of £2,600 − £2,080 = £520 is the tax relief (20% of £2,600) that she obtained when making the payments.

The income tax computation in this case follows the same principles as it did in Task 1:

Analysis of Taxable Income (as previously):	£
General Income (£15,000 + £38,000 − £10,000)	43,000
Savings Income	10,000
Dividend Income	6,000
	59,000

Because of the payments under gift aid and to the personal pension plan, the basic rate band is now extended by (£1,000 + £1,600) from £31,865 to £34,465 cumulative.

This is used as follows:

Income Tax Calculation:

General Income:	£	£
£34,465 x 20%	6,893.00	
£8,535 x 40%	3,414.00	
£43,000		10,307.00
Savings Income:		
£10,000 x 40% (all in this band)	4,000.00	
		4,000.00
Dividend Income:		
£6,000 x 32.5% (all in this band)	1,950.00	
		1,950.00
Income Tax Liability		16,257.00
Less Paid		2,600.00
Income Tax to Pay		13,657.00

In this situation Dee now has to pay £13,657.

This compares with a payment of £14,177 in Task 1, a tax saving of £520 (20% of £2,600), which when added to the £520 tax relief given on the payments (see above) gives a total tax saving of £1,040 (£2,600 x 40%).

PERSONAL ALLOWANCES FOR OLDER PEOPLE

We noted in Chapter 1 that there are different personal allowances for those born before 6/4/1948. We will now look at these in more detail. The full allowances for 2014/15 are as follows:

Basic allowance – born after 5/4/48	£10,000
Age-related allowance – born between 6/4/38 and 5/4/48	£10,500
Age-related allowance – born before 6/4/38	£10,660

There is an income limit for age-related allowances, so that only those with income at or below the limit will obtain the full allowances quoted above. For 2014/15 the income limit is £27,000.

The income that is compared to this limit is calculated as follows:

Total Income (ie before deducting any personal allowance)	£xxxxx
Less grossed-up gift aid payments (if any)	£(xxxxx)
Less grossed-up personal pension payments (if any)*	£(xxxxx)
Income for comparison with limit	£xxxxx

*Although personal pension contributions are less likely for those in this age group, they are possible.

If the taxpayer's income (using this calculation) exceeds the limit of £27,000, then the age-related allowance is reduced by 50% of the difference. This restriction cannot, however, reduce the allowance below the basic allowance of £10,000, unless the income is over £100,000 (see next section).

This is a little complicated, so we will illustrate it with some examples.

example

Bill, born in 1945, has total income of £27,500. He makes no payments to gift aid or personal pension contributions.

His age-related allowance would be calculated as follows:

	£
Age-related allowance – born between 6/4/38 and 5/4/48	10,500
Less restriction 50% x (£27,500 – £27,000)	250
Allowance	10,250

The tax computation would then be worked out in the normal way, using the allowance of £10,250.

We will use some slightly more complex figures for the next example.

example

Brenda, born in 1935, has total income of £32,000. She makes a £400 (net) payment to gift aid, but no personal pension contributions.

Brenda's income (for comparison with the limit) is calculated as:

	£
Total Income	32,000
Less grossed-up gift aid payments (£400 x 100/80)	500
Income for comparison with limit	31,500

Her age-related allowance would be calculated as follows:

	£
Age-related allowance – born before 6/4/38	10,660
Less restriction 50% x (£31,500 – £27,000)	2,250
	8,410
But allowance cannot be less than	10,000

Brenda will therefore have an allowance of £10,000.

You can see from the way that the calculation works that no one with substantial income would benefit from age-related allowances.

Case Study

PENSIONER PETE: AGE-RELATED ALLOWANCES

Pete was born in 1930. During the tax year he had income from pensions totalling £27,000, and received dividends of £1,800. He made gift-aid payments of £600 (net). He had tax of £3,400 deducted from his pension income.

required

(a)   Calculate the age-related allowance for Pete

(b)   Use this to calculate the tax payable or refundable

solution

(a) Pete's income (for comparison with the limit) is calculated as:

	£
Total Income (£27,000 + (£1,800 x 100/90))	29,000
Less grossed-up gift aid payments (£600 x 100/80)	750
Income for comparison with limit	28,250

His age-related allowance would be calculated as follows:

	£
Age-related allowance – born before 6/4/38	10,660
Less restriction 50% x (£28,250 – £27,000)	625
Allowance	10,035

(b) Tax computation 2014/15

	£	£
		Tax Paid
Employment Income (Pensions)	27,000	3,400
Dividends	2,000	200
Total Income	29,000	3,600
Less Personal Allowance	10,035	
Taxable Income	18,965	

Analysis of taxable income:	
General Income	16,965
Dividend Income	2,000
	18,965

Although the basic rate band would be increased by the grossed-up amount of gift aid, Pete does not have enough income to benefit from this. Note that the income for comparison with the allowance limit is not the same amount as that used in the income tax computation.

Income tax Calculation:

		£
General Income	£16,965 x 20%	3,393.00
Dividend Income	£2,000 x 10%	200.00
Income tax liability		3,593.00
less paid		3,600.00
Income tax to be refunded		(7.00)

PERSONAL ALLOWANCES FOR INDIVIDUALS WITH HIGH INCOMES

When an individual has income over £100,000 the personal allowance can be restricted or eliminated entirely. This works in a similar way to the allowance restriction for older people as examined in the previous section, but there is no lower limit to the allowance.

The income that is used to compare with the £100,000 limit is calculated in the same way as we saw in the last section:

Total income (before deducting any personal allowance)	£xx
Less grossed-up gift aid payments (if any)	£(xx)
Less grossed-up personal pension payments (if any)	£(xx)
'Adjusted Net Income' for comparison with limit	£xx

If the taxpayer's adjusted net income exceeds the £100,000 limit, then the personal allowance is reduced by 50% of the difference. This means that an individual with adjusted net income of £120,000 or more would not be entitled to any personal allowance at all.

example

Jim has employment income of £95,000, plus dividends received of £13,500. He pays £2,000 per year (net) to charities under gift-aid.

Jim's adjusted net income would be:

£95,000 + (£13,500 x 100/90) − (£2,000 x 100/80) = £107,500

This exceeds the £100,000 limit by £7,500, so Jim's personal allowance will be reduced by 50% x £7,500 = £3,750. His personal allowance will therefore be £10,000 − £3,750 = £6,250.

If Jim's income had been £120,000 or more then 50% of the excess over £100,000 would eliminate the personal allowance entirely. Note however that the allowance cannot be less than zero. There cannot be a negative personal allowance.

This system also applies to those born before 6/4/48. If they had income of over £100,000 it would already be too high to benefit from the increased age allowance, and they would be treated in an identical way to younger taxpayers.

TAX RATES FOR INDIVIDUALS WITH HIGH INCOMES

We noted in earlier chapters that there is an 'additional rate' band that impacts on individuals who have taxable income of over £150,000. The rates that apply are 45% for general and savings income, and 37.5% for dividend income.

An individual with taxable income of over £150,000 will suffer the elimination of the personal allowance as explained in the last section. Although there is an extra tax band to use in the computation, the calculation follows the same principle that we have used throughout our studies. We must analyse the income into general, savings and dividend income, and then work our way up through the bands, applying the appropriate rates.

Case Study

HIGH INCOME COMPUTATION

Julie has the following income in the tax year:

	£
Trading income	140,000
Interest received (net)	16,000
Dividends received	27,000

Her income tax computation for 2014/15 would appear as follows:

	£	Tax Paid £
Trading Income	140,000	
Interest	20,000	4,000
Dividends	30,000	3,000
Total Income	190,000	7,000
Less Personal Allowance	0	
Taxable Income	190,000	

The taxable income is easily analysed since there is no personal allowance:

	£
General	140,000
Savings	20,000
Dividends	30,000

Working up through the bands:

	£	£
General Income:		
£31,865 x 20%	6,373	
£108,135 x 40%	43,254	
£140,000		49,627
Savings Income:		
£10,000 x 40%	4,000	
£10,000 x 45%	4,500	
£20,000		8,500
Dividend Income:		
£30,000 x 37.5%	11,250	
		11,250
Total Tax Liability		69,377
Less Tax Paid		7,000
Tax Payable		62,377

The following diagram (which is not to scale) illustrates the calculation:

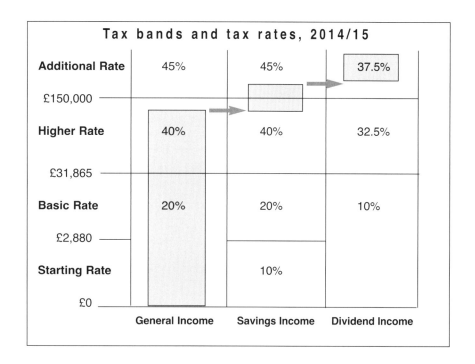

Where an individual makes gift aid and/or personal pension contributions, both the band limits of £31,865 and £150,000 are increased by the gross equivalent of the payments, and the taxpayer will therefore get increased tax relief on the payments.

example

If a taxpayer with a income of £165,000 (all general income) made gift aid payments of £8,000, the band limits would both be increased by £8,000 x 100/80 = £10,000. This would mean that the basic rate band would extend to £41,865, and the higher rate band would reach £160,000. In this situation the individual would pay tax as follows:

		£
£41,865	x 20%	8,373
£118,135	x 40%	47,254
£5,000	x 45%	2,250
£165,000		57,877

COMPREHENSIVE TAX COMPUTATIONS

We have now examined all the issues that we need to understand to produce comprehensive income tax computations. All the topics covered in the following Case Study have been looked at already in this book, and it should therefore provide a good way of starting revision.

Case Study

MAX CASE:
COMPREHENSIVE TAX COMPUTATION

Max received rent from furnished property in the tax year of £10,800. He paid out allowable expenses of £500 in relation to the property, and also intends to claim wear and tear allowance. He has £750 of losses from property income carried forward from the previous tax year.

Max is employed as a senior manager, at a basic gross salary of £85,000 per year. Out of this his employer deducts £100 per month contribution to an approved pension scheme. Max paid £28,000 under PAYE.

He is also provided with a petrol engine company car. It had a list price of £15,600 when new, and has an emission rating of 215 grams of carbon dioxide per kilometre. Max is entitled to fuel for the car paid for by his employer for business and private motoring. Max pays an annual subscription of £130 to the Association of Company Administrators (an approved professional body).

Max has various investments, and during the tax year he received £1,080 dividends from UK companies, plus £1,120 interest (after deduction of tax) from his bank accounts.

Max made a £400 donation to charity under the gift aid scheme during the tax year. Max uses paper-based tax returns.

required

1   Calculate the assessable property income.

2   Calculate the assessable employment income.

3   Calculate the assessable savings and dividend income and the tax that has effectively been paid on this.

4   Calculate the personal allowance for Max.

5   Using an income tax computation, calculate the total tax liability for the tax year, and the amount that has yet to be paid.

6   State the date by which the final tax payment must be made, and the final date for submitting Max's 2014/15 tax return.

solution

We will deal with each task in turn, selecting the appropriate data. In this Case Study the information is provided in the same order as the tasks to make the process clearer.

Task 1

Property Income	£
Rental received	10,800
less	
allowable expenditure	500
wear & tear allowance (£10,800 x 10%)	1,080
	9,220
less loss brought forward	750
Assessable amount	**8,470**

Task 2 £

Employment Income	
Basic salary	85,000
less pension contribution	1,200
Salary per P60	83,800
add benefits:	
Company car (£15,600 x 35%)	5,460
Company car fuel (£21,700 x 35%)	7,595
	96,855
less allowable expenses (professional fees)	130
Assessable amount	**96,725**

Task 3

Savings and Dividend Income

	Amount Rec'd	Tax	Assessable
	£	£	£
Bank Interest	1,120	280	1,400
Dividends	1,080	120	1,200

Task 4

	£
Total Income:	
Property Income	8,470
Employment Income	96,725
Savings Income	1,400
Dividend Income	1,200
	107,795
Less grossed-up gift aid payment	500
'Adjusted Net Income'	107,295

This exceeds the £100,000 limit by £7,295. The personal allowance is therefore reduced by 50% of this excess:

	£
Basic personal allowance	10,000
less 50% x £7,295	3,647
Revised personal allowance	6,353

Task 5   **Income Tax Computation 2014/15**

	£	£ Tax Paid
Property Income	8,470	-
Employment Income	96,725	28,000
Savings and Investment Income:		
(interest rec'd)	1,400	280
(dividend income)	1,200	120
Total Income	107,795	28,400
Less Personal Allowance	6,353	
Taxable Income	101,442	

Analysis of Taxable Income:	
General Income (£8,470 + £96,725 − £6,353)	98,842
Savings Income	1,400
Dividend Income	1,200
	£101,442

The basic rate band will be increased by the gross equivalent of the gift aid payment (£400 x 100/80 = £500).

This makes the new top of the band £31,865 + £500 = £32,365.

The income level does not reach the additional rate band.

Income Tax Calculation:

General Income:	£	£
£32,365 x 20%	6,473.00	
£66,477 x 40% (the rest of the £98,842)	26,590.80	
		33,063.80
Savings Income (£1,400 x 40%)		560.00
Dividend Income (£1,200 x 32.5%)		390.00
Income tax liability		34,013.80
less paid		28,400.00
Balance to pay		5,613.80

Task 6

Final payment must be made by 31/1/16, and the paper-based tax return must be filed by 31/10/15.

COMPLETING THE TAX RETURN

Once the full computation has been finalised, and all the assessable figures and claims entered onto the tax return (including the supplementary pages) the taxpayer needs to sign the tax return (if it is paper-based) or submit the online version.

HMRC will calculate the tax if the paper-based form is submitted on time and notify the taxpayer of the amount payable or repayable. There is no longer a box on the main tax return to enter the amount of tax due, although a 'tax calculation summary' is available on request for a taxpayer to complete if they wish.

If the online tax return version is submitted the software will automatically calculate the amount of tax and offer a printout of the computation.

A REVIEW OF PAYMENT DATES

In Chapter 1 we saw that the final date for payment of income tax is 31 January following the end of the tax year (eg 31/1/16 for 2014/15). We also discussed briefly the timing of payments on account that are sometimes due. We will now look a little more closely at these advance payments.

payments on account

The two payments on account are calculated as follows:

Each payment on account is based on half the income tax amount due for the previous year, (after deducting tax paid under PAYE and other income tax deducted at source).

Suppose, for example, the total income tax for 2013/14 was £7,000, of which £4,000 had been paid via PAYE. Each of the two payments on account for 2014/15 would be:

$$\frac{£7,000 - £4000}{2} = \frac{£3,000}{2} = £1,500$$

These payments on account for 2014/15 would be made on
- 31 January 2015
- 31 July 2015

If the amount of income tax paid each year is quite similar, there would not be much left to pay (or have refunded) on the final date of 31 January 2016.

Payments on account do not have to be made if **either**
- the amount of tax payable the previous year was less than £1,000 (excluding tax deducted at source), or
- more than 80% of the tax due the previous year was collected at source

Suppose, for example, the total income tax for 2013/14 was £7,000 of which £5,900 had been paid by PAYE, leaving £1,100 payable. Even though this is over the £1,000 limit, payments on account for 2014/15 would not be needed as £5,900 is more than 80% of the £7,000 total.

Payments on account can also be reduced or eliminated if the taxpayer makes a claim that their tax for the coming year will be less than for the previous year.

INTEREST AND PENALTIES

interest payable

Interest is payable on late payment of tax, and also on any underpayment of the amount due on account. The rates are different to those used for assessing beneficial loans. The rate is 3.0% at the time of going to press.

penalties

Late submission of the tax return:

■ a £100 penalty for missing the deadline – regardless of the amount of tax involved

■ for returns over 3 months late – an additional daily penalty of £10 per day up to a 90 day maximum of £900

■ for returns over 6 months late – an additional £300 or 5% of the tax due if this is higher

■ for returns over 12 months late – a further £300 or 5% of the tax due if this is higher. In serious cases the penalty could be up to 100% of the tax due instead

There are very limited 'reasonable excuses' for late returns; for example a fire or flood destroying paperwork, or a serious illness.

If a tax return has not been submitted by the deadline, HMRC may estimate the amount of tax due. This estimate can only be changed by the submission of a tax return.

Late payment of the balancing payment by more than 30 days:

■ 5% of the tax due, plus

■ a further 5% of the tax due if the balancing payment is still unpaid by 31 July (ie 6 months late)

■ a third 5% of the tax due if payment has still not been made 12 months after it was due

Note that the penalties are in addition to the interest charges.

These penalties do not apply to payments on account which are paid late, only to balancing payments for the tax year.

incorrect returns

If, after submitting a tax return, the taxpayer discovers that he/she has made an error or omission, he/she should notify HM Revenue & Customs as soon as possible. If the alteration results in less tax being payable than was originally thought, the taxpayer will receive a refund. Where additional tax is due this will of course need to be paid, plus interest that will run from the normal payment date.

The following penalty system applies where error(s) or omissions by the taxpayer result in too little tax being assessed. This system also applies when a taxpayer has failed to notify HMRC about a source of taxable income.

The level of penalty is based on whether the error has been caused by carelessness by the taxpayer, or is more serious.

If the error is:

Due to **lack of reasonable care**, the penalty will be between 0% and 30% of the extra tax due,

Deliberate, the penalty will be between 20% and 70% of the extra tax due, and if

Deliberate and concealed, the penalty will be between 30% and 100% of the extra tax due.

The percentage can be reduced if the taxpayer tells HMRC about the error(s), helps them work out the extra tax, and gives HMRC access to check the figures.

The following diagram shows the range of possibilities in more detail. An 'unprompted' disclosure is where the taxpayer tells HMRC about the inaccuracy that he has no reason to believe HMRC has discovered, or are about to discover. All other disclosure is considered 'prompted'.

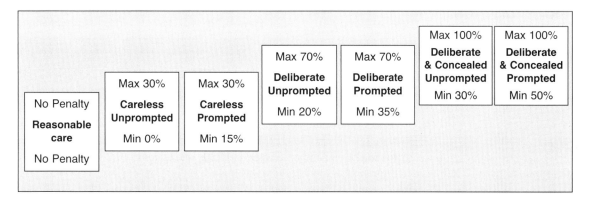

time limits for assessments and claims

If a taxpayer (or his agent) finds that they have made a mistake on a tax return they have normally got 12 months from 31 January following the end of the tax year to correct it. For the tax year 2014/15 amendments can therefore be made by 31 January 2017. If the return was submitted online it can also be amended online within the above dates. If a paper return was submitted, then a complete amended paper return must be sent in.

You may recall that this is the same time limit for elections like claiming wear and tear allowance or rent a room relief in connection with property income.

HMRC can still be told about errors after the above date, but then they must be notified to HMRC in writing. Such notifications must be made within four years of the end of the tax year. This means the deadline relating to the tax year 2014/15 is 5 April 2019.

The same four year limit applies to HMRC when they discover taxpayers' errors (as discussed in the last section), provided the taxpayer has taken reasonable care. If the errors are the result of careless behaviour by the taxpayer the time limit is six years, and if the taxpayer's behaviour was deliberate the time limit is twenty years.

Chapter Summary

- The income tax computation is used to bring together income from various sources and calculate the tax. We have studied in some detail income from property, income from savings and investments, together with income from employment. We only need to have an outline understanding of profits from self-employment or partnership (trading income).

- Income tax is calculated by working up through the bands, looking at general income, followed by savings income, and finally dividend income. Each of these classifications of income use their own tax rates.

- Payments to charities under the gift aid scheme, and to pension providers for personal pension plan contributions are made net, which provides tax relief at basic rate. Further tax relief is provided for higher and additional rate taxpayers by increasing the basic rate tax band by the gross amounts of these types of payment.

- Higher personal allowances are available for those born before 6 April 1948. The higher allowances are subject to income limit calculations.

- Individuals (of any age) with income over £100,000 are subject to the restriction or elimination of their personal allowance.

- Final payment of tax is due by 31 January following the end of the tax year. Some taxpayers are also required to make estimated payments on account based on the previous year's tax amount. Payments on account are due on the 31 January in the tax year, plus the 31 July following the tax year.

- Penalties are payable for late submission of returns, and interest and penalties are payable for late balancing payments. Late payments on account will incur interest but not penalties.

Key Terms

Gift Aid

a scheme whereby individuals can make payment(s) to charities as net amounts, and the charity can claim the income tax back; higher rate taxpayers get further relief through their tax computations

Personal pension plan

a type of pension plan (including a stakeholder pension) arranged for an individual – basic rate tax relief is provided by making payments net of 20% income tax while higher rate and additional rate taxpayers get further relief through their tax computations

Activities

5.1 Jo paid £2,000 (net) under the gift aid scheme and £3,040 (net) to her pension provider as personal pension plan contributions. Her total taxable pay is £50,000 (all general income).

Calculate:

(a) the gross equivalent of each payment

(b) the effective cost to her of each payment, after taking into account higher rate tax relief

5.2 Matt has the following assessable income for the tax year:

Rental Income	£9,400
Employment Income	£26,500 (tax paid under PAYE £3,300)
Gross Interest Received	£5,000 (tax deducted £1,000)
Dividends + Tax Credits	£12,000

He paid £2,400 (net) to a personal pension plan during the tax year.

Required:

(a) Using an income tax computation, calculate the income tax liability and the amount of tax that is outstanding.

(b) Calculate whether any payments on account are required for the next tax year, and if so how much would need to be paid, and when. Round payments on account down to £.

5.3 John had a balance of income tax to pay for 2014/15 of £400. However he did not send in his online tax return or pay this amount until 31/3/16.

Assume that the HM Revenue & Customs interest rate is 3.0%. Interest calculations can be made on a monthly basis.

Calculate (in £) the total interest and penalties due.

5.4 Mike received rent from furnished property in 2014/15 of £6,300. He paid out insurance of £350 in relation to the property, and also intends to claim wear and tear allowance. He has £250 of losses against property income carried forward from the previous year.

Mike is employed as an accountant, at a gross salary of £148,500 per year. He paid £48,220 under PAYE in 2014/15.

Mike uses his own car for occasional company business trips. During 2014/15 he travelled 2,000 business miles, and was reimbursed by his employer at 80p per mile. Mike paid his membership fees of £205 to the ACCA.

Mike has various investments, and during the tax year he received £1,260 in dividends from UK companies, plus £800 interest (after deduction of tax) from his bank accounts.

Required:

(a)   Calculate the assessable property income.

(b)   Calculate the assessable employment income.

(c)   Calculate the assessable savings and dividend income, and the tax that has effectively been paid on this.

(d)   Using an income tax computation, calculate the total tax liability for 2014/15, and the amount that has yet to be paid.

(e)   State the date by which the final tax payment must be made, and the final date for submitting his 2014/15 paper-based tax return.

5.5   During 2014/15, Rachel, who was born in 1945, had income of £26,000 and received dividends of £936.

Required:

Calculate her total income tax liability (ie before deduction of tax paid) for 2014/15, using the table given below.

	£
Income	
Gross dividends	
Personal allowance	
Taxable income	

5.6   Steve has written to you with the following query:

"I am writing to you for some clarification on my father's tax affairs. He is no longer capable of handling his own money, and I have a letter of authorisation allowing me to deal with his tax matters.

"I have received notification from HMRC of how much tax he has to pay on 31 January 2015. It says he owes £1,400 from 2013/14, and needs to pay £3,500 for 2014/15. I thought he had paid all the tax due for 2013/14, so I don't understand what the £1,400 is for. Also, I know that he has hardly any income this tax year, so where does the £3,500 come from?

"If you could explain the system to me, it would be much appreciated."

Required:

Respond appropriately to his query.

5.7   During the tax year, Robert had employment income of £89,000 and received dividends of £18,000. He paid £2,400 (net) into a personal pension scheme.

Calculate his total income tax liability (ie before deduction of tax paid), using the table given below.

	£
Employment Income	
Gross dividends	
Personal allowance	
Taxable income	

6 Capital gains tax – the main principles

this chapter covers...

In this chapter we introduce the second of the two taxes that we study in this unit – capital gains tax (CGT). This is a tax on the gains made on disposal on capital assets, and we will define a disposal, before examining which assets are chargeable and which are exempt.

We will then see how capital gains tax is calculated, by using the annual exemption and the appropriate rate of tax.

Next we look in detail at the calculations of each gain or loss, including the special rules that apply to spouses, civil partners and connected persons. In this section we learn what expenses can form allowable deductions in our calculations.

Losses and how they are relieved are examined next, and we will see how they are first set against the gains of the same tax year, before being carried forward if necessary.

We round off the chapter with a comprehensive case study to illustrate the issues already covered and consolidate our understanding.

AN INTRODUCTION TO CAPITAL GAINS TAX

Capital Gains Tax (CGT) applies in certain circumstances to individuals who dispose of capital assets that they have previously acquired. It often applies to the sale or gift of an asset that may have been owned for quite some time. This can result in what is called a 'chargeable gain'. Note that CGT does not apply to trading assets, where items are regularly bought and sold to make a profit, as these are not classed as capital assets.

Although capital gains tax applies to both personal assets and business assets, we are only going to examine how it applies to personal assets in this book. Gains on the disposal of business assets are dealt with in the unit 'Business Tax' (see Osborne Books' *Business Tax*).

basis of assessment

Capital gains tax is applied to individuals by using the same tax years as those used for income tax. The basis of assessment for capital gains tax is the **chargeable gains less capital losses** arising from disposals that occur during the tax year.

We will look at how losses are dealt with later in this chapter. The main issues to understand at this point are that the tax is based on the total (or aggregate) of gains that have occurred, and that a gain can only arise when a **disposal** has taken place.

disposals

A disposal arises when an asset is

- sold (or part of it is sold), or
- given away, or
- lost, or
- destroyed

Most of the situations that we will come across will be based on the sale or gift of an asset. You should remember, however, that a disposal can also result from loss or destruction of an asset. In the case of loss and destruction, the value of the asset is most likely to be assessed as zero, unless insurance proceeds are received.

Two special situations where disposals do not give rise to capital gains tax are:

- disposals arising because the owner has died, and
- any disposal between spouses (husband and wife) or civil partners

CHARGEABLE AND EXEMPT ASSETS

For capital gains tax to arise, the asset that has been disposed of must be a 'chargeable' asset. Exempt assets are entirely outside the CGT system. Instead of there being a long list of the assets that are chargeable, there is a fairly short list of assets that are exempt.

The simple rule is that if an asset is not exempt, then it must be chargeable!

A list of the main exempt assets is set out below:

exempt assets

- principal private residence – an individual's home (we will look at the rules for this later)
- cars
- wasting chattels (chattels are tangible, movable items; wasting means they have an estimated life of less than 50 years). Items of machinery for personal use (including, for example, clocks) are normally considered wasting chattels
- chattels bought and sold for £6,000 or less (there are also some special rules for those sold for more than £6,000 that we will look at later)
- Government Securities (Gilts)
- gifts made to charity
- shares that are held in a NISA

chargeable assets

Some typical personal assets that are chargeable and regularly feature in examination tasks include:

- antique furniture and paintings (since they have already lasted over 50 years)
- holiday homes
- land (eg a field not part of a main residence)
- shares

You must remember that these are only examples – all assets are chargeable unless they are exempt.

CALCULATION OF CAPITAL GAINS TAX

All individuals are entitled to an annual exempt amount – an **annual exemption** – for each tax year. This works in a similar way to a personal allowance under income tax. The exempt amount is deducted from the total net gains that have been calculated on the individual assets that have been disposed of during the year. Capital gains tax is then worked out on the balance.

The exempt amount is £11,000 in 2014/15. The exempt amount can only be used against capital gains (not set against income), and cannot be carried back or forward and used in another tax year.

Once the exempt amount has been deducted from the total net gains, the balance is subject to Capital Gains Tax at 18%, or 28% or a combination of these two rates.

Although Capital Gains Tax is a separate tax from Income Tax, it uses the same band structure. Gains are treated as if they were added on top of taxable income, and the 18% rate is applied to gains falling within the basic rate band and the 28% rate applies to gains within the higher or additional rate bands.

The following diagram (which is an extended version of the one used earlier to illustrate income tax bands, and is not to scale) shows how the system works.

Tax bands and tax rates, 2014/15

	General Income	Savings	Dividends	Capital Gains Tax
Additional Rate	45%	45%	37.5%	
£150,000				
Higher Rate	40%	40%	32.5%	28%
£31,865				
Basic Rate	20%	20%	10%	18%
£2,880				
Starting Rate		10%		
£0				

Income Tax

If an individual is already a higher rate or additional rate taxpayer then any gains will always be taxed at 28%. Where the taxpayer pays income tax only at the basic rate (or the starting rate) then any gains will be taxed at 18% provided they do not exceed the basic rate band of £31,865 when added to taxable income. Where they do exceed this amount the excess will be taxed at 28%. The following example will illustrate the situation.

example

Rashid has total taxable general income of £30,000 after deducting his personal allowance. He made capital gains of £25,000 before deducting his exempt amount.

Rashid has taxable gains of £25,000 – £11,000 (exempt amount) = £14,000. He has £31,865 – £30,000 = £1,865 remaining in his basic rate band after accounting for his taxable income. Therefore £1,865 of his gains will be taxed at 18%, and the remainder taxed at 28%, as follows:

£1,865 x 18%	£335.70
£12,135 (the remainder of the £14,000) x 28%	£3,397.80
Total Capital Gains Tax	£3,733.50

We must now turn our attention to how to calculate the chargeable gain or loss on each separate disposal.

THE COMPUTATION OF EACH GAIN

Each disposal of a chargeable asset requires a calculation to determine the amount of any gain or loss. This computation follows a standard format that is in effect a mini income statement (profit & loss account) for the item disposed of. There are some minor variations to this format in particular circumstances, as we will see later. The basic format is as follows:

	£
Proceeds on disposal	X
less	
Incidental costs of disposal	(x)
Net proceeds	X
less	
Original cost	(x)
Incidental costs of acquisition	(x)
Gain (or loss)	X

proceeds on disposal

This normally refers to the amount that the asset realised when it was disposed of – ie the selling price. However there are some special situations where the figure used is different:

- if the asset was given away (to anyone), or sold to a 'connected' person at less than the market value, the **market value** is used in the computation instead of the actual amount received. A chargeable gain can therefore arise even though the person disposing of the asset has received no proceeds

- if the asset has been lost or destroyed then the asset will have been disposed of for zero proceeds, and zero will be used in the computation – and there could be a loss. The exception to this would be if an insurance claim has been made, in which case the amount of the claim proceeds would be used

transfer to spouse or civil partner

When an asset is transferred to a spouse or civil partner no capital gain arises, as mentioned earlier. This is achieved by treating the disposal proceeds as the amount needed to generate exactly zero gain or loss.

For example if a wife had bought an asset some time ago for £10,000, (with no other costs) and gave it to her husband, the disposal proceeds would be treated as £10,000 so that no gain would arise. This would also mean that if the husband later sold the asset, his cost would also be considered to be £10,000, and any gain calculated on that basis.

A transfer between spouses or civil partners is often known as being made on a 'no gain, no loss' basis.

transfer to 'connected person'

As already noted, when an asset is sold to a connected person at less than market value, the market value is used in the computation of gains.

The following relatives of the person disposing of the asset are 'connected persons', and so are the relatives' spouses or civil partners:

- ancestors and spouse's ancestors (parent, grandparent, etc)
- siblings and spouse's siblings (brother, sister)
- lineal descendants and spouse's lineal descendants (child, grandchild etc)

So, for example the following people **would** each be a **connected person**, and any disposal would be deemed to be at market value:

- brother's wife
- wife's grandfather
- daughter's husband

Each of the following people (for example) **would not** be a **connected person**:

- uncle or aunt
- cousin
- friend

Remember that **gifts** (whether to a connected person or not) are always deemed to be a disposal at market value, unless they are to a spouse or civil partner.

If a loss is incurred on a disposal to a connected person, the loss cannot be set against general gains, but can only be set against gains made on other disposals to the same person.

incidental costs of disposal

Incidental costs are the costs incurred by the taxpayer in selling the asset. Examples include advertising expenses, auction costs, or estate agent's fees for selling a property.

original cost, and incidental costs of acquisition

This relates to the amount paid to acquire the asset in the first place, plus any other costs incurred to buy it. Examples of these costs would include legal fees or auction costs. If the asset was given or bequeathed to the taxpayer, the market value at that time is used. We will examine in the next chapter how to deal with expenditure incurred later to improve the asset.

Case Study

HOLLY DAY:
COMPUTATION OF GAIN

Holly bought a cottage in Cornwall in August 1990 to use for her holidays. She paid £59,000 for the cottage, and also paid legal fees of £1,000 at the same time to arrange the purchase.

In the current tax year Holly sold the cottage for £240,000. The estate agent's fees for the sale were £3,000, and she incurred further legal fees of £2,000.

The cottage was Holly's only disposal of a chargeable asset during the tax year.

Holly is a higher rate income tax payer.

required

Calculate the gain on the disposal of the cottage, and the amount of Capital Gains Tax that Holly must pay.

solution

	£
Proceeds on disposal	240,000
less	
Incidental costs of disposal	(5,000)
Net proceeds	235,000

less	
Original cost	(59,000)
Incidental costs of acquisition	(1,000)
Gain	175,000

	£
Total gains for the tax year	175,000
Less exempt amount	(11,000)
Subject to CGT	164,000

Capital Gains Tax
£164,000 x 28% = £45,920

Holly pays CGT at 28% because she is already a higher rate taxpayer under Income Tax.

DEALING WITH LOSSES

Capital losses arise from disposals in the same way as gains.

When losses have been calculated they are dealt with as follows:

- they are firstly set against gains arising in the same tax year, until these are reduced to zero, then
- any unused loss is carried forward to set against the next gains that arise in future tax years – at this stage the annual exempt amount can be safeguarded

We will now use an example to illustrate how this works.

example

Kulvinder has the following capital gains and losses, based on disposals occurring in 2012/13, 2013/14 and 2014/15.

	2012/13	2013/14	2014/15
	£	£	£
Gains	20,000	17,000	28,000
Losses	(35,000)		

For our calculations here, we will assume that the annual exempt amount remains at £11,000 for each of these three years.

required

Calculate how the loss can be used to offset the gains, and the amount subject to CGT each year.

2012/13

Because the loss of £35,000 occurred in the same year as the gain of £20,000, we must set off as much loss as possible against the gain, until the net gain is reduced to zero. There is no CGT liability in 2012/13. We then carry the loss balance of (£35,000 – £20,000 = £15,000) on to the next year.

2013/14

We now have a brought forward loss, and can offset it against the 2013/14 gains. However because the loss is brought forward we only need to use up enough loss to bring the net gain down to the exempt amount.

We therefore use up £6,000 of the brought forward loss – just enough to bring the net gains for this year down to the exempt amount. There is no CGT liability in 2013/14, and a loss of (£15,000 – £6,000 = £9,000) to carry forward to 2014/15.

2014/15

This year the remaining loss of £9,000 that has been brought forward is set against the gain of £28,000. From the balance of £19,000 is deducted the exempt amount of £11,000, leaving £8,000 that is subject to tax.

summary

	2012/13	2013/14	2014/15
	£	£	£
Losses working			
Loss brought forward	0	15,000	9,000
Loss incurred	35,000	0	0
Loss used up	20,000	6,000	9,000
Loss carried forward	15,000	9,000	0
Calculation of gains			
Gains	20,000	17,000	28,000
Loss set off	(20,000)	(6,000)	(9,000)
Net gains	0	11,000	19,000
Less exempt amount		(11,000)	(11,000)
Amount subject to CGT	0	0	8,000

Now apply what you have learnt about capital gains so far by working through the comprehensive Case Study that follows.

Case Study

IVOR LOTT:
CAPITAL GAINS TAX PRINCIPLES

Ivor Lott made the following disposals during the tax year. Ivor has taxable income of £20,000 (after deducting his personal allowance).

- He sold his entire holding of 3,000 shares that he owned in Expo Limited for £6.75 each. He had bought all the shares in August 1998 for £10.00 each.

- He sold an antique table for £15,000 that he had bought in July 1996 for £7,000.

- He gave his daughter a field that was located 3 miles away from his home. He bought the field in April 1985 for £2,000. It was valued at £150,000 at the time of the gift, since it was now a possible housing development site.

- He sold his Jaguar E type car for £25,000. He had owned the car since January 1983 when he had bought it for £5,000.

- He sold his holiday cottage in Cornwall for £200,000. He incurred selling costs of £5,000. He had bought the cottage in April 2002 for £152,000, and incurred buying costs of £8,000.

required

- Calculate any gain or loss on each disposal.
- Calculate the capital gains tax payable by Ivor for the tax year (to the nearest £).

solution

Shares in Expo Limited

	£
Proceeds (3,000 x £6.75)	20,250
less cost (3,000 x £10)	(30,000)
Capital loss	(9,750)

Antique table

Proceeds	15,000
less cost	(7,000)
Gain	8,000

Field

Market Value	150,000
less cost	(2,000)
Gain	148,000

A gain arises even though Ivor received no proceeds.

Car

This asset is exempt from capital gains tax.

Holiday Cottage

Proceeds on disposal	200,000
less	
Incidental costs of disposal	(5,000)
Net proceeds	195,000
less	
Original cost	(152,000)
Incidental costs of acquisition	(8,000)
Gain	35,000

We can now add together the gains, and offset the loss.

	£
Gains:	
Antique table	8,000
Field	148,000
Holiday cottage	35,000
	191,000
less loss on shares	(9,750)
Net gains	181,250
less exempt amount	(11,000)
Subject to CGT	170,250

Capital Gains Tax

	£
£11,865* x 18%	2,135.70
£158,385 x 28%	44,347.80
£170,250	46,483.50

* £31,865 – £20,000 taxable income

Chapter Summary

■ Capital gains tax is assessable on individuals who dispose of chargeable assets during the tax year. A disposal usually takes the form of the sale or gift of the asset. All assets are chargeable unless they are exempt. Exempt assets include principal private residences, cars, government securities (gilts), and certain chattels.

■ Each disposal uses a separate computation that compares the proceeds or market value with the original cost of the asset.

■ Losses are set off against gains. An annual exempt amount is deductible from the net gains The balance is taxed at 18% or 28% depending on the individual's income.

Key Terms

Capital Gains Tax (CGT) a tax that applies to individuals who dispose of chargeable assets – it is charged at 18% or 28%

disposal a disposal for CGT purposes is the sale, gift, loss or destruction of an asset

chargeable asset this term is used to describe assets whose disposal can result in a CGT liability – all assets are chargeable unless they are exempt

exempt asset an asset that is not chargeable to CGT: exempt assets include principal private residences, cars, gilts, and some chattels

chattel a tangible, movable asset – ie the majority of personal possessions

wasting chattel a chattel with an expected life of fewer than 50 years

annual exempt amount

the amount (also known as the 'annual exemption') that is deductible from an individual's net gains in a tax year before CGT is payable – the amount is £11,000 in 2014/15

net proceeds

the proceeds from the sale of an asset, less any incidental costs of selling the asset

capital loss

a capital loss results when the allowable costs of an asset exceed the sale proceeds (or market value). A loss is used by setting it against a gain in the same year, or if this is not possible, by carrying the loss forward to set against gains in the next available tax year

connected person

normally a close relative; sales to a connected person at less than market value are deemed to be at market value

Activities

6.1   Analyse the following list of assets into those that are chargeable to CGT and those that are exempt.

(a)   an antique painting sold for £10,000

(b)   an individual's second home, used for weekends away

(c)   Shares in CIC plc

(d)   an individual's only home

(e)   a small yacht

(f)   an antique bed, bought for £500, and sold for £2,000

(g)   a car

(h)   Government securities

6.2   Josie had a capital gain on her only disposal in the tax year of £15,000. Her taxable income is £22,000.

Calculate the amount of Josie's Capital Gains Tax liability for the tax year.

6.3   Tariq had a capital gain on one disposal in 2014/15 of £35,000, and on the only other disposal, a capital loss of £9,000. His taxable income is £28,000 (after deducting personal allowance).

Calculate the amount of Tariq's Capital Gains Tax liability for the tax year.

6.4   April bought a holiday cottage in May 1995 for £60,000 and sold it in the current tax year for £130,000. She had no other disposals in the current tax year. April is a higher rate income tax payer.

Calculate April's CGT liability for the tax year.

6.5   Cliff bought a holiday flat in August 1998 for £50,000 and sold it in January 2015 for £165,000. In the same month he sold some shares for £32,000 which he had bought in July 2004 for £52,000. Cliff has taxable income of £35,000.

Calculate Cliff's CGT liability for the tax year.

6.6   Ivan Asset has capital losses brought forward from the previous tax year of £15,000. He made the following disposals during the tax year.

He sold his entire holding of 5,000 shares that he owned in Astro plc for £12.00 each. He had bought all the shares in June 1998 for £8.00 each.

He sold his Morgan car for £15,000. He had owned the car since January 1999 when he had bought it for £29,000.

He sold an antique dresser for £14,000 that he had bought in July 1996 for £9,000.

He gave his son 4,000 shares in Expo Ltd. He bought all the shares in January 1995 for £2.00 each. The shares were valued at £5 each at the time of the gift.

Ivan is a higher rate income tax payer.

Required:

(a) Calculate any gain or loss arising from each of the disposals.

(b) Calculate the amount of Capital Gains Tax payable for the tax year.

6.7 Justin Shaw has capital losses brought forward from the previous tax year of £18,000. He made the following disposals during the tax year. Justin's taxable income is £25,000:

He sold his yacht for £12,000. He had owned it since January 2001 when he had bought it for £23,000.

He sold his entire holding of 1,000 shares that he owned in Captain plc for £15.00 each. He had bought all the shares in June 1997 for £9.00 each.

He sold an antique painting of a ship for £14,000 that he had bought in July 1984 for £10,000.

He gave his daughter 3,000 shares in Boater Ltd. He bought all the shares in January 1996 for £3.00 each. The shares were valued at £7 each at the time of the gift.

Required:

(a) Calculate any gain or loss arising from each of the disposals.

(b) Calculate the amount of Capital Gains Tax payable for the tax year.

6.8 For each statement, tick the appropriate box.

		Actual proceeds used	Deemed proceeds used	No gain or loss basis
(1)	Grandfather gives an asset to his granddaughter	☐	☐	☐
(2)	Wife gives an asset to her husband	☐	☐	☐
(3)	Steve sells an asset to his friend for £13,000 when the market value is £16,000	☐	☐	☐
(4)	Mary sells an asset to her son's wife for £20,000 when the market value is £60,000	☐	☐	☐
(5)	Sue gives an asset to her civil partner, April	☐	☐	☐

6.9 **(1)** Andrew bought an asset in January 2000 for £26,000, selling it in December 2014 for £45,000. He paid auctioneers commission of 3% when he bought the asset and 5% when he sold the asset.

The gain on this asset is:

✔

(a) £20,470	
(b) £15,970	
(c) £17,530	
(d) £19,000	

(2) True or false: advertising costs are not an allowable deduction as they are revenue expenses.

6.10 State which of the following statements are true:

(1) The annual exemption is applied before capital losses are deducted.

(2) Excess capital losses cannot normally be set against other taxable income.

(3) Capital gains are taxed at 20% for basic rate tax payers.

7 Capital gains tax – some special rules

this chapter covers...

In this final chapter we learn about some rules which apply to certain special situations. These diverse situations are brought together here just because special rules apply.

We start by learning how to calculate gains or losses when only part of an asset has been disposed of and the remaining part is kept. We use cost apportionment based on valuations at the date of sale to do this.

We then see how capital improvement (or 'enhancement') expenditure can form an allowable cost in the gains computation.

Next we examine the rather complicated rules surrounding principal private residence relief that apply when a property is not occupied throughout its ownership.

The subsequent section deals with shares and the special rules relating to matching, pooling, and bonus and rights issues.

We finally examine the payment of CGT, the completion of the return, and the keeping of records.

DEALING WITH PART DISPOSALS

We saw in the last chapter that a disposal for Capital Gains Tax (CGT) purposes can relate to all or part of an asset. Although part disposal will not apply to many assets that are not divisible, it could apply (for example) to a piece of land.

If an asset was acquired as a whole, and then part of it is sold while the rest is retained, we need to compute the gain (or loss) on the part that was disposed of. The difficulty is that although we know how much the proceeds are for that part of the asset, we probably don't know how much of the original cost of the whole asset relates to that portion.

The way that this issue is tackled is to value the remaining part of the asset at the time of the part disposal. The original cost can then be apportioned by using these figures.

The cost applicable to the part disposed of is:

$$\text{Original cost of whole asset} \quad \times \quad \frac{A}{(A + B)}$$

where   A = Proceeds (or market value) of part disposed of, and

B = Market value of part retained

The following example will illustrate the calculation.

example

Heather bought a large field for £4,000 in January 1991 to keep her horses. In the current tax year she sold a part of the field for £3,000. At the same time the remainder of the field was valued at £9,000.

The portion of the original cost relating to the part of the field that was sold would be calculated as:

$$£4,000 \quad \times \quad \frac{£3,000}{(£3,000 + £9,000)}$$

This gives the cost as $£4,000 \times \dfrac{3,000}{12,000} = £1,000$.

The computation would then be carried out in the normal way:

	£
Proceeds	3,000
less cost (as calculated)	(1,000)
Gain	2,000

IMPROVEMENT EXPENDITURE

Where expenditure after acquisition is incurred to enhance an asset, and it is then disposed of in this improved condition, the improvement expenditure forms an allowable cost in the computation.

The expenditure must be of a 'capital' nature, and examples of this could include extending a building or having an antique professionally restored.

The following example illustrates the situation:

example

Sonny Daze bought a holiday cottage for £60,000 in September 1984. In January 1990 he spent £40,000 extending the property. He sold the cottage in the current tax year for £300,000.

		£
Proceeds		300,000
less	original cost	(60,000)
	improvement expenditure	(40,000)
Gain		200,000

PRINCIPAL PRIVATE RESIDENCES

We saw in the last chapter that a taxpayer's only or main residence – known as a principal private residence (PPR) – is exempt from Capital Gains Tax. Properties that have never been used as a main residence (for example holiday homes) are fully chargeable.

Where a taxpayer has two properties, and uses them both as main residences, only one can be treated as a PPR, and the taxpayer can elect as to which one it is. The election must be made to HMRC within two years of aquiring the second property. This could occur, for example, if a taxpayer used a property near his workplace during the week and another property situated elsewhere at weekends.

A property's status may change if it is occupied as a PPR for only part of its period of ownership. If this happens and the property is subsequently disposed of a gain can arise. In these circumstances the gain is worked out initially based on the whole period of ownership, and then apportioned to arrive at the exempt gain by multiplying the total gain by:

$$\frac{\text{period of occupation (as a PPR)}}{\text{period of ownership}}$$

Provided a property has been a PPR for some time during its ownership then the last 18 months of ownership are always regarded as part of the PPR occupation period. This is the case even if there is another PPR in use during that time.

We will now illustrate this using an example:

example

James bought a cottage in the Lake District for £50,000 on 1 January 1988 to use as a holiday home. He retired on 1 January 1998, and decided to sell his PPR and move into the cottage. On 1 January 2003 he bought a house in the Cotswolds as his PPR, moved there and went back to using the Lake District cottage as a holiday home.

On 1 January 2015 he sold the cottage in the Lake District for £250,000.

We first calculate the gain based on the whole period of ownership.

	£
Proceeds	250,000
less cost	(50,000)
Gain for whole period	200,000

We then time apportion the gain, counting the last 18 months of ownership as occupation, regardless of whether it actually was.

Owned: 1/1/88 - 1/1/15 = 27 years = 324 months

Actually occupied as PPR: 1/1/98 - 1/1/03 = 5 years = 60 months

Deemed occupation as PPR: 1/7/13 - 1/1/15 = 1½ years = 18 months

Total actual and deemed occupation = 78 months

Exempt gain: £200,000 x 78/324 = £48,148

Chargeable gain: £200,000 x 246/324 = £151,852

In addition to the above rule, there are other periods of absence that will count as being occupied as a PPR, provided:

- the property was **actually occupied** as a PPR at some time both **before** and **after** the period, and

- no other property is being treated as a PPR during the period of absence

These additional periods of 'deemed occupation' are:

- three years in total for any reason,

- up to four years when the taxpayer is absent due to UK employment,

- any period when the taxpayer is living abroad due to employment

Case Study

LOVELY MOVER: PRINCIPAL PRIVATE RESIDENCE

Simon Lovely bought a house in London on 1 July 1990 for £50,000. He lived in it as his principal private residence (PPR) until 1 January 1998 when he started a new job in Scotland. He rented a flat in Edinburgh to live in, but he kept his London house. On 1 July 2007, he left his job in Scotland, and moved back into his London house. On 1 January 2009 he bought a house in Cornwall, which he elected to be his PPR and moved out of his London house. On 1 July 2014, he sold his London house for £510,000.

He made no other disposals in the tax year. Simon is a higher rate income tax payer.

required

- Calculate the chargeable gain on disposal of the London house.

- Calculate the capital gains tax payable by Simon for the year.

solution

	£
Sale proceeds	510,000
less cost	(50,000)
Gain before PPR relief	460,000

	Ownership (Years)	Actual/deemed occupation (Years)
Actual Occupation 1/7/90 - 1/1/98	7.5	7.5
Working in UK 1/1/98 - 1/7/07	9.5	7 *(see next page)
Actual Occupation 1/7/07 - 1/1/09	1.5	1.5
Absence 1/1/09 - 1/7/14	5.5	1.5 (last 1.5 years)
Total ownership	24	
Actual/deemed occupation		17.5

*The deemed occupation periods for 'working elsewhere in the UK' (4 years maximum) and 'absence for any reason' (3 years maximum) can both be claimed making a total of 7 years.

		£
Exempt gain	460,000 x 17.5/24 =	335,417
Chargeable gain	460,000 x 6.5/24 =	124,583

	£
Gain	124,583
Annual exemption	(11,000)
Amount subject to capital gains tax	113,583

Capital gains tax £113,583 x 28% = £31,803.24

SPECIAL RULES FOR CHATTELS

Chattels are tangible, moveable items such as furniture, jewellery, works of art and vehicles. As we saw in the last chapter, certain chattels are entirely exempt from Capital Gains Tax. These exempt chattels are:

- wasting chattels (those with an expected life of less than 50 years)
- cars
- chattels that are both bought and sold for £6,000 or less

There are also some special rules about the amount of gain or loss that can occur when chargeable chattels are disposed of. Although these rules are not particularly complicated, they do need to be remembered.

chattels sold at a gain for over £6,000

In this situation the gain is limited to an amount of:

5/3 (Proceeds – £6,000)

The 'proceeds' in this calculation is the gross proceeds – the amount received before deducting any selling expenses.

This is sometimes known as the 'chattel marginal relief'.

Suppose gains had been calculated on disposals as follows:

Disposal A

Proceeds	£9,000
Cost	£1,500
Gain	£7,500

The gain would be restricted to 5/3 (£9,000 – £6,000)   = £5,000

£5,000 would therefore be used as the gain figure, since it is less than the £7,500 based on the normal calculation.

Disposal B

Proceeds	£9,000
Cost	£6,500
Gain	£2,500

Here the gain would also be restricted to £5,000, but since the calculated gain is only £2,500 the restriction would have no effect. The £2,500 gain would therefore stand.

chattels sold at a loss for less than £6,000

If the chattel had also been bought for less than £6,000 the transaction would be exempt from CGT. If the chattel had been acquired for over £6,000 then the loss would be limited by substituting £6,000 for the actual proceeds in the calculation.

For example a chattel bought for £8,000 and sold for £3,000 would have a loss calculated as:

	£
Deemed proceeds	6,000
less actual cost	(8,000)
Loss	(2,000)

Make sure that you understand this process, and remember that it is the proceeds that are deemed to be £6,000. This is an area where it is easy to get confused if you are not careful.

We will now use a Case Study to help consolidate our understanding of the main issues that we have covered in this chapter so far.

Case Study

JUSTIN CREASE:
USING SPECIAL RULES

Justin made the following disposals. He is a higher rate income tax payer.

- He sold an antique lamp for £7,500. The lamp had cost £4,200 when he bought it in January 1999.

- He sold part of a large field for £10,000. He had bought the whole field in January 1990 for £8,000. At the time of the sale the market value of the remaining part of the field was £30,000.

- He sold a house in September 2014 for £325,000. He had bought the house in January 1998 for £160,000, and immediately used it as his main residence. He bought a new house in April 2013, and nominated that as his PPR. He rented out the original house from April 2013 until it was sold.

- He sold his gold cufflinks for £5,000. They had been left to him in his Uncle's will in September 1995. The value of the cufflinks at that time was £7,800.

- He bought an antique painting in January 1990 for £25,000. In September 1995 he paid £15,000 to have it professionally restored. The restored painting was sold for £90,000.

required

- Calculate the gain or loss on each applicable disposal.
- Calculate the amount of Capital Gains Tax that Justin will have to pay in respect of the tax year.

solution

Antique Lamp £

Proceeds	7,500
less cost	(4,200)
Gain	3,300

but gain restricted to:

5/3 (£7,500 – £6,000) = £2,500

Field

Proceeds	10,000
less apportioned cost:	
£8,000 x £10,000 / (£10,000 + £30,000)	(2,000)
Gain	8,000

House

The house is entirely exempt. The period when it was rented out still counts as being occupied, as it is less than 18 months, and occurs at the end of the ownership period.

Cufflinks £

Deemed proceeds	6,000
less value at acquisition	(7,800)
Loss	(1,800)

Antique painting

Proceeds	90,000
less: cost	(25,000)
improvement expenditure	(15,000)
Gain	50,000

We can now add together the gains, and set off the loss.

	£
Gains:	
Antique Lamp	2,500
Field	8,000
Antique painting	50,000
	60,500
less loss on cufflinks	(1,800)
Net gains	58,700
Less exempt amount	(11,000)
Subject to CGT	47,700

Capital Gains Tax
£47,700 x 28% = £13,356

MATCHING RULES FOR SHARES

We saw in the last chapter that shares are chargeable assets, and that the computation for the acquisition and subsequent disposal of a block of shares is the same as for other assets.

The complication that can arise is when various quantities of the same type of share in the same company are bought and sold. The problem faced is similar to that in any stock valuation situation – how to determine which of the shares that were bought are deemed to be the same ones that were sold. The dilemma is solved in this situation by the application of strict **matching rules**.

When some shares are sold the matching process is carried out by working down the following categories of acquisition, skipping any that do not apply, until all the shares sold have been matched. A separate CGT computation is then used for each separate match.

1   Firstly, any shares bought on the **same day** that the disposal occurs are matched with that disposal.

2   Secondly, any shares bought in the **30 days after** the disposal are matched with those disposed of, (matching the earliest first if more than one acquisition). This probably seems illogical – selling something before it is bought!

3   Thirdly, any remaining shares not yet matched are deemed to have come from the 'FA 1985 pool' of shares. This is a device for merging shares.

The above order of matching is illustrated in the diagram below. The numbers in the diagram relate to the numbered stages described above.

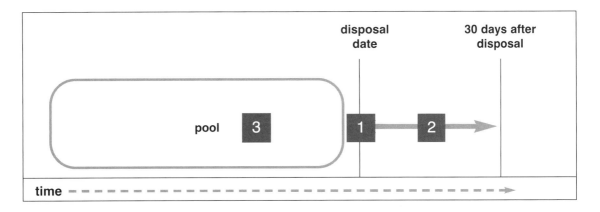

Remember that this matching process only applies where there have been several purchases of the same type of shares in the same company. It does not apply to a mixture of different companies shares, nor is it needed where a shareholding is bought and sold intact.

USING THE 'FA 1985 POOL'

This device was introduced in the 1985 Finance Act, and merges (or 'pools') shares in the same company and of the same type together. As we just saw, it occurs as the last of the matching rules, and is used to calculate the cost of shares acquired before the disposal date.

It is similar to the calculation of weighted average inventory valuations (as you have probably studied in Costing).

The pool needs to keep data relating to:

- numbers of shares and
- actual costs

These form the two main columns of the pool working.

The pool commences with the first shares bought. It then moves forward in time, adding each subsequent purchase of shares to provide cumulative numbers and costs of shares in the pool.

When any shares from the pool are disposed of, a proportion of the cumulative cost at the time of disposal is deducted from the pool, based on the numbers of shares. This cost amount that is deducted from the pool is then used in the gains calculation and compared with the proceeds in the normal way.

We will now demonstrate how the process works using a numerical example.

example

On 1/1/2015 Julie sold 10,000 ordinary shares in WyeCo Ltd for £10 each, from her shareholding of 25,000. Her shareholding had been built up as follows:

1/1/1988 bought 17,000 shares for £5.00 each

1/1/1993 bought 8,000 shares for £7.00 each.

Since there are no acquisitions on or after 1/1/2015, the whole of the disposal of 10,000 shares will be matched with the pool. The pool will be built up as follows, with the disposal deducted as the latest transaction:

	Number	Cost
		£
1/1/1988 Purchase	17,000	85,000
1/1/1993 Purchase	8,000	56,000
Pool Totals	25,000	141,000
Less Disposal	(10,000)	(56,400)
Pool Balance after disposal	15,000	84,600

You should note the following:

- the cost figures for the disposal are a proportional amount of the pool costs before disposal, based on the number of shares (e.g. £141,000 x 10,000 / 25,000 = £56,400)

The computation for the disposal will now appear as follows:

	£
Proceeds (10,000 x £10)	100,000
Less cost	(56,400)
Gain	43,600

If at some future date there was another disposal of shares from the pool then the pool balance remaining (as on the previous page) would be used to determine the cost of the shares in the further disposal.

BONUS AND RIGHTS ISSUES

dealing with bonus shares

Bonus shares are additional shares given free to shareholders based on their current shareholding. This is sometimes called a 'scrip issue' and may be carried out as part of a capital restructuring of the company.

For CGT purposes the bonus shares are treated as if they were acquired at the same time as the original shares that generated the issue. For example a shareholder who owned 1,000 shares that were bought in January 2001 would be entitled to a further 200 shares if, later on, there were a bonus issue of 'one for five' shares. The total of 1,200 shares would be treated as bought in January 2001 for the amount paid for the 1,000 shares.

In virtually all situations, bonus shares are added to the pool when they are received. Since no payment is made, there is no adjustment to the cost figure.

If the bonus shares are received based on several acquisitions of original shares, the bonus shares will still be added into the pool, since the original shares will also be in the pool.

dealing with rights issues

A **rights issue** is the situation where additional shares are sold to existing shareholders, usually at a special price. For matching purposes, the shares that are bought in this way are treated as if they were bought with the original shares.

Rights issue shares will join the pool and be treated like any other share purchase. Their cost will be added into the pool.

We will now use a case study to make sure the principles relating to various matters studied are clear.

Case Study

CHER BYERS:
GAINS INCLUDING SHARES AND POOLING

Cher had acquired the following quoted ordinary shares in AbCo Plc (a listed company).

1/5/1985	1,000 shares at £4.00 each	£4,000
1/1/1990	Bonus issue of 1 for 4	
1/1/1992	1,750 shares at £4.20 each	£7,350
1/1/1995	1,500 shares at £4.10 each	£6,150 (Rights issue)
1/12/2001	1,800 shares at £5.10 each	£9,180

On 15/11/2001 she had sold 1,000 of her shareholding.

On 15/8/2014 she sold a further 2,500 ordinary shares in AbCo Plc for £10.00 each.

Cher also made the following disposals during 2014/15:

- she sold a plot of land for £20,000. This originally formed part of a larger field that she bought for £15,000 in January 1992. At the time of the sale the remaining portion of land was valued at £40,000

- she sold an antique ring for £6,600. She had bought it on 1 January 1999 for £3,500

- she sold an antique painting for £10,000. She had bought it in December 1996 for £14,000

Cher has taxable income of £29,000 (after deducting her personal allowance).

required

1   Identify which shares would have already been matched against the disposal that took place on 15/11/2001.

2   Show how the disposal of shares on 15/8/2014 will be matched against the acquisitions, and

3   Calculate the total gain arising from the sale of shares that took place on 15/8/2014.

4   Calculate any gains or losses arising from the disposal of the other assets.

5   Calculate the total Capital Gains Tax payable in respect of the tax year.

solution

1

The disposal of 1,000 shares on 15/11/2001 would have been matched with 1,000 of the 1,800 shares that were bought on 1/12/2001 for £5.10 each (shares bought in the 30 days after disposal). This leaves 800 of that purchase to join the pool.

2

Matching of the 15/8/2014 disposal of 2,500 shares will be entirely against the pool, since there were no shares of that type bought on that date or the following 30 days.

3

We will first need to build up the pool to August 2014, so that we can calculate the balances.

		Number	Cost
			£
1/5/1985	Purchase	1,000	4,000
1/1/1990	Bonus Issue	250	-
1/1/1992	Purchase	1,750	7,350
1/1/1995	Rights Issue	1,500	6,150
1/12/2001	Balance of Purchase (1,800 less 1,000 already matched)	800	4,080
		5,300	21,580
15/8/2014	Disposal	(2,500)	(10,179) *
	Pool balance after disposal	2,800	11,401

* The cost of the shares disposed of is calculated as:
(2,500 / 5,300) x £21,580 = £10,179

We can now calculate the gain on the disposal of shares, using the cost figure calculated in the pool.

	£
Proceeds	25,000
less cost	(10,179)
Gain	14,821

4

This task involves the computations on other asset disposals.

Land

	£
Proceeds	20,000
less apportioned cost:	
£15,000 x £20,000 / £60,000	(5,000)
Gain	15,000

Antique Ring

	£
Proceeds	6,600
less cost	(3,500)
Provisional gain	3,100

Gain is limited to 5/3 (£6,600 − £6,000) = £1,000

Antique Painting

	£
Proceeds	10,000
less cost	(14,000)
Loss	(4,000)

5

	£
Gains:	
Shares	14,821
Land	15,000
Antique ring	1,000
	30,821
Less loss on antique painting	(4,000)
Net gains	26,821
Less exempt amount	(11,000)
Subject to CGT	15,821
Capital Gains Tax	
£2,865 x 18%	515.70
£12,956 x 28%	3,627.68
	4,143.38

PAYMENT OF CAPITAL GAINS TAX

Capital Gains Tax is payable by individuals by the 31 January following the tax year in which the gains took place. It is payable at the same time (using a combined payment slip) as the balancing Income Tax payment for the same tax year. There is no system of payments on account for CGT.

COMPLETING THE CGT SECTION OF THE TAX RETURN

The Capital Gains Tax pages of the tax return are a supplementary section, consisting of pages CG1 and CG2.

The form is a summary of the gains and losses, and would be submitted together with the actual computations.

We will use the data from the last Case Study to show how the form works.

Note that the 2014/15 version of the form was not available when this book was published, so the 2013/14 version is used instead.

CHER BYERS:
COMPLETING THE CGT PAGES

Cher Byers had various disposals in the tax year and has an amount of £15,821 subject to CGT (see previous page).

required

Using the data from the Case Study, complete pages CG1 and CG2 from the tax return.

solution

The completed pages are shown on the next pages. We have used the 2013/14 version of the form, as the 2014/15 version was not available when this book was published. The following notes should help you to follow the completion of the form.

Boxes 3 to 17 are a summary, with additional detail included in later boxes.

Box 3 shows the total of any gains made in the year, before either any losses or the annual exempt amount have been deducted.

Box 6 shows the amount of any losses incurred in the year – here the £4,000 relates to the loss incurred on the antique painting. Any losses brought forward and used would be inserted into box 7.

The other boxes in the summary section refer to adjustments and use of losses that do not apply here.

On page CG2, boxes 18 to 23 are for disposals of shares in listed companies. We have one disposal – the shares in AbCo plc, and boxes 18 to 21 refer to that disposal.

Unlisted shares disposals would be entered into the next section, and all other disposals into the final section. Here we have three disposals (the land, ring and painting), and the figures in boxes 31-33 refer to these. Note that only gains on these disposals are summarised in box 33 – any losses are ignored in this box.

There may well be boxes with descriptions that you are not familiar with, but don't panic. If the issues have not been covered in this book then you can assume that the box will not need to be completed.

HM Revenue & Customs

Capital gains summary
Tax year 6 April 2013 to 5 April 2014

1 Your name

C H E R   B Y E R S

2 Your Unique Taxpayer Reference (UTR)

Summary of your enclosed computations

Please read the *Capital gains summary notes* before filling in this section. **You must enclose your computations, including details of each gain or loss, as well as filling in the boxes.**

To get notes and helpsheets that will help you fill in this form, go to hmrc.gov.uk/selfassessmentforms

3 Total gains *(Boxes 21 + 27 + 33 + 34)*
£ 30 821 · 0 0

4 Gains qualifying for Entrepreneurs' Relief (but excluding gains deferred from before 23 June 2010) – *read the notes*
£ · 0 0

5 Gains invested under Seed Enterprise Investment Scheme and qualifying for exemption – *read the notes*
£ · 0 0

6 Total losses of the year – *enter '0' if there are none*
£ 4 0 0 0 · 0 0

7 Losses brought forward and used in the year
£ · 0 0

8 Adjustment to Capital Gains Tax – *read the notes*
£ − · 0 0

9 Additional liability for non-resident or dual resident trusts
£ · 0 0

10 Losses available to be carried forward to later years
£ · 0 0

11 Losses used against an earlier year's gain (special circumstances apply – *read the notes)*
£ · 0 0

12 Losses used against income – amount claimed against 2013-14 income – *read the notes*
£ · 0 0

13 Amount in box 12 relating to shares to which Enterprise Investment Scheme/Seed Enterprise Investment Scheme relief is attributable
£ · 0 0

14 Losses used against income – amount claimed against 2012-13 income – *read the notes*
£ · 0 0

15 Amount in box 14 relating to shares to which Enterprise Investment Scheme/Seed Enterprise Investment Scheme relief is attributable
£ · 0 0

16 Income losses of 2013-14 set against gains
£ · 0 0

17 Deferred gains from before 23 June 2010 qualifying for Entrepreneurs' Relief
£ · 0 0

Listed shares and securities

18 Number of disposals - *read the notes*

`1`

19 Disposal proceeds

£ `2 5 0 0 0 · 0 0`

20 Allowable costs (including purchase price)

£ `1 0 1 7 9 · 0 0`

21 Gains in the year, before losses

£ `1 4 8 2 1 · 0 0`

22 If you are making any claim or election, put 'X' in the box

23 If your computations include any estimates or valuations, put 'X' in the box

Unlisted shares and securities

24 Number of disposals - *read the notes*

25 Disposal proceeds

£ `· 0 0`

26 Allowable costs (including purchase price)

£ `· 0 0`

27 Gains in the year, before losses

£ `· 0 0`

28 If you are making any claim or election, put 'X' in the box

29 If your computations include any estimates or valuations, put 'X' in the box

Property and other assets and gains

30 Number of disposals

`3`

31 Disposal proceeds

£ `3 6 6 0 0 · 0 0`

32 Allowable costs (including purchase price)

£ `2 2 5 0 0 · 0 0`

33 Gains in the year, before losses

£ `1 6 0 0 0 · 0 0`

34 Attributed gains where personal losses cannot be set off

£ `· 0 0`

35 If you are making any claim or election, put 'X' in the box

36 If your computations include any estimates or valuations, put 'X' in the box

Any other information

37 Please give any other information in this space

KEEPING RECORDS

Since capital gains occur when assets that may have been held for a considerable time are disposed of, this has implications for record keeping. Taxpayers need to plan ahead, and retain records relating to the acquisition of assets that will be chargeable if disposed of.

Typical records that should be kept include:

- contracts, invoices or other purchase documentation relating to the acquisition of assets
- schedules of purchase and disposal of shares and securities
- details of any valuations (eg for assets acquired from a deceased's estate, and valuations relating to part disposals)
- documentation relating to the sale of assets

Records for CGT purposes should be retained for the same period of time as those relating to Income Tax. This is one year after the date that the online return must be submitted (eg for 2014/15 records should be kept until 31/01/17). Where records will also relate to later disposals, for example share pool data and information relating to part disposals, they will need to be retained until all the relevant assets have been disposed of.

Chapter Summary

- This chapter deals with separate special rules for various circumstances.

- The cost of a part disposal is calculated by apportioning the cost of the whole asset. This is carried out by using the proceeds of the part disposed of as a proportion of the value of the whole asset at the time of disposal.

- Improvement expenditure that is reflected in the asset when disposed of is an allowable cost.

- Principal private residences are exempt assets provided they are occupied as such during the whole ownership. Certain periods of absence are treated as deemed periods of occupation. Where there are periods of absence that do not fall under these special rules, the exempt part of the gain on the property is calculated as a proportion of the whole gain, based on the period of occupation as a fraction of the period of ownership.

- Chattels that are acquired and sold for under £6,000 are exempt. Where they are sold at a gain for over £6,000 the gain is restricted to 5/3 of the gross proceeds minus £6,000. Where sold at a loss for under £6,000, the loss is restricted by substituting £6,000 for the actual proceeds in the computation.

- When shares of the same type in the same company are bought and sold at different times matching rules are used to identify the shares disposed of. Firstly shares bought on the day of disposal are matched. Secondly those bought in the 30 days after disposal are matched. Thirdly any earlier acquisitions are pooled and matched. This is known as the FA 1985 pool.

- Bonus and rights issues are treated as acquired at the time of the shares that they are derived from for matching purposes. They normally appear as part of the FA 1985 pool.

- Capital Gains Tax is payable by 31 January following the end of the tax year. The gains section of the tax return summarises the computations.

- Records must be kept relating to both the acquisition and disposal of chargeable assets. Due to the nature of the assets this may involve retaining documentation for a considerable time.

Key Terms

part disposal	occurs when part of an asset is disposed of, but the remainder is retained
improvement expenditure	capital expenditure that enhances an asset – if the enhancement is still evident at disposal, then the improvement expenditure is an allowable cost
deemed occupation	periods of absence from a Principal Private Residence that are treated as periods of occupation for CGT purposes
chattels	tangible, moveable assets
wasting chattels	chattels with an expected life of less than fifty years
matching rules for shares	rules which determine which acquisitions of shares are identified with each disposal
bonus shares	extra shares given to shareholders in proportion to their current shareholding
rights issue	shares sold to existing shareholders at a special preferential price

Activities

7.1   Alice made the following disposals in the tax year. She is a higher rate income tax payer.

She sold part of a piece of land for £30,000 that she had bought in January 1992. The whole piece of land had cost her £50,000 at that time. At the time of the sale the remaining land was valued at £120,000.

She sold her holiday cottage for £300,000 that she had bought for £60,000 in September 1985. She had also spent £50,000 in January 1992 extending the cottage.

Required:

Calculate the total capital gains tax for Alice for the tax year.

7.2   Bertie made the following disposals in the tax year. Bertie's taxable income is £20,000.

He sold an antique painting for £20,000 that he had bought for £5,000 in January 1992. He had the painting professionally restored in January 1995, and this cost £6,000.

He sold an antique table for £7,800. The table had been bought in January 1990 for £1,400.

Selling costs were £100.

Required:

Calculate the total capital gains tax for Bertie for the tax year.

7.3   Christine made the following disposals in the tax year.

She gave her sister an antique necklace that she had bought for £5,000. The necklace was valued at £8,000 at the time of the gift.

She sold her Jaguar E type car for £18,000. She had bought the car for £6,000, and spent £10,000 having it professionally restored.

On 31/12/2014 she sold her house in Dorking for £470,000. The house had been bought for £80,000 on 1/1/1988. Her use of the house was as follows:

1/1/1988 - 31/12/1997	occupied as Christine's PPR
1/1/1998 - 31/12/1999	rented out as Christine went on a world holiday
1/1/2000 - 31/12/2008	occupied as Christine's PPR
1/1/2009 - 31/12/2014	rented out as Christine moved to a new PPR.

Christine's taxable income is £30,000.

Required:

Calculate the total capital gains tax for Christine for the tax year.

7.4 David made the following disposals in the tax year. He is a higher rate income tax payer.

He sold 14,400 of his ordinary shares in Zydeco Ltd on 30/07/2014 for £72,000 in total. His shareholding in this company had been built up as follows:

1/1/1992   Bought 3,000 shares for £3.00 each.

1/1/1999   Bought 12,000 shares for £3.50 each.

1/1/2000   Bought rights issue shares on the basis of 1 for 5 at the price of £2.00 each.

David sold an antique dresser for £6,900. The dresser was bought for £3,000 in January 2000.

Required:

Calculate any gain made on

- the disposal of shares in July 2014, and
- the disposal of the dresser

Calculate the amount of any CGT that will be payable.

7.5 Edward is a higher rate income tax payer. Edward had acquired the following quoted ordinary shares in Exray Plc (a listed company):

1/5/1985	1,000 shares	£ 8,000
1/1/1992	1,750 shares	£15,750
1/1/1995	1,500 shares	£10,650 (Rights issue)
1/12/2001	1,800 shares	£18,360

On 15/11/2001 he sold 2,000 of his shareholding.

On 15/7/2014 he sold a further 2,500 ordinary shares in Exray Plc for £12.00 each.

Edward also made the following disposals during the tax year:

- he sold a plot of land for £20,000. This originally formed part of a larger field that he bought for £5,000 in January 1988. At the date of disposal the remaining portion of land was valued at £80,000
- he sold an antique brooch for £9,600. He had bought it on 1 January 1999 for £5,500
- he sold an antique table for £12,000. He had bought it on 1 December 1999 for £13,500

Required:

1 Identify which shares would have already been matched against the disposal that took place on 15/11/2001.

2 Show how the disposal of shares on 15/7/2014 will be matched against the acquisitions, and

3 Calculate the total gain arising from the sale of shares that took place on 15/7/2014.

4 Calculate any gains or losses arising from the disposal of the other assets.

5 Calculate the total Capital Gains Tax payable in respect of the tax year.

6 Complete pages CG1 and CG2 of the tax return for Edward (see next two pages for the 2013/14 version).

Capital gains summary
Tax year 6 April 2013 to 5 April 2014

HM Revenue & Customs

1	Your name		2	Your Unique Taxpayer Reference (UTR)

Summary of your enclosed computations

Please read the *Capital gains summary notes* before filling in this section. **You must enclose your computations, including details of each gain or loss, as well as filling in the boxes.**

ℹ️ To get notes and helpsheets that will help you fill in this form, go to hmrc.gov.uk/selfassessmentforms

3 Total gains *(Boxes 21 + 27 + 33 + 34)*
£ · 0 0

4 Gains qualifying for Entrepreneurs' Relief (but excluding gains deferred from before 23 June 2010) - *read the notes*
£ · 0 0

5 Gains invested under Seed Enterprise Investment Scheme and qualifying for exemption - *read the notes*
£ · 0 0

6 Total losses of the year - *enter '0' if there are none*
£ · 0 0

7 Losses brought forward and used in the year
£ · 0 0

8 Adjustment to Capital Gains Tax - *read the notes*
£ · 0 0

9 Additional liability for non-resident or dual resident trusts
£ · 0 0

10 Losses available to be carried forward to later years
£ · 0 0

11 Losses used against an earlier year's gain (special circumstances apply - *read the notes)*
£ · 0 0

12 Losses used against income – amount claimed against 2013-14 income - *read the notes*
£ · 0 0

13 Amount in box 12 relating to shares to which Enterprise Investment Scheme/Seed Enterprise Investment Scheme relief is attributable
£ · 0 0

14 Losses used against income – amount claimed against 2012-13 income - *read the notes*
£ · 0 0

15 Amount in box 14 relating to shares to which Enterprise Investment Scheme/Seed Enterprise Investment Scheme relief is attributable
£ · 0 0

16 Income losses of 2013-14 set against gains
£ · 0 0

17 Deferred gains from before 23 June 2010 qualifying for Entrepreneurs' Relief
£ · 0 0

Listed shares and securities

18 Number of disposals - *read the notes*

19 Disposal proceeds

£ [   ] · 0 0

20 Allowable costs (including purchase price)

£ [   ] · 0 0

21 Gains in the year, before losses

£ [   ] · 0 0

22 If you are making any claim or election, put 'X' in the box

23 If your computations include any estimates or valuations, put 'X' in the box

Unlisted shares and securities

24 Number of disposals - *read the notes*

25 Disposal proceeds

£ [   ] · 0 0

26 Allowable costs (including purchase price)

£ [   ] · 0 0

27 Gains in the year, before losses

£ [   ] · 0 0

28 If you are making any claim or election, put 'X' in the box

29 If your computations include any estimates or valuations, put 'X' in the box

Property and other assets and gains

30 Number of disposals

31 Disposal proceeds

£ [   ] · 0 0

32 Allowable costs (including purchase price)

£ [   ] · 0 0

33 Gains in the year, before losses

£ [   ] · 0 0

34 Attributed gains where personal losses cannot be set off

£ [   ] · 0 0

35 If you are making any claim or election, put 'X' in the box

36 If your computations include any estimates or valuations, put 'X' in the box

Any other information

37 Please give any other information in this space

7.6   Robert bought a house on 1 February 2000 for £70,000. He lived in the house until 31 January 2005 when he moved in with his elderly parents. The house remained unoccupied until he sold it on 1 July 2014 for £205,000. This house is Robert's only property.

(a)   Which periods are treated as occupied and which are not?

Occupation / Deemed Occupation	Non-occupation

(b)   What is the chargeable gain on the property?

7.7   The following table relates to sales of chattels

Match the statements shown below to the correct asset details.

Asset	Sale proceeds	Cost	Statement
1	£4,000	£3,000	
2	£12,000	£8,000	
3	£7,000	£5,000	
4	£3,000	£8,000	
5	£15,000	£21,000	

Statements:

Exempt asset

Calculate gain as normal

Calculate loss as normal

Sale proceeds to be £6,000

Chattel marginal relief applies

Answers to activities

CHAPTER 1: INTRODUCTION TO INCOME TAX

1.1   The following statements are true: (a), (e), (f). The other statements are false.

1.2   Income Tax Computation for Mary

	£	£
		Tax Paid
Trading Income	2,800	-
Employment Income	12,300	460
Property Income	4,500	-
Total Income	19,600	460
Less Personal Allowance	10,000	
Taxable Income	9,600	
Income Tax Calculation:		
£9,600 x 20%	1,920.00	
Income Tax Liability	1,920.00	
Less already paid	460.00	
Income tax to pay	1,460.00	

Note

The trading income is based on the accounting year to 30/9/14, because it ends in the tax year 2014/15.

The employment income is based on the amount received in the tax year, irrespective of the period that it relates to.

1.3   **(a)**   Dividend Income, part of Savings and Investment Income

(b)   Employment Income – full title Employment, Pensions and Social Security Income

(c)   Exempt

(d)   Savings Income, part of Savings and Investment Income

(e)   Exempt

(f)   Property Income

1.4 Income Tax Computation for John

	£	£
		Tax Paid
Employment Income	7,920	0
Property Income	3,000	-
Total Income	10,920	0
Less Personal Allowance	10,000	
Taxable Income	920	
Income Tax Calculation:		
£920 x 20%	184.00	
Income Tax Liability	184.00	
Less already paid	0.00	
Income tax to pay	184.00	

Note

The property income includes the March rent since it operates on an accruals basis.

The interest on a NISA is exempt.

1.5 Income Tax Computation for Megan

	£	£
		Tax Paid
Trading Income	14,700	-
Employment Income	34,400	4,880
Total Income	49,100	4,880
Less Personal Allowance	10,000	
Taxable Income	39,100	
Income Tax Calculation:		
£31,865 x 20%	6,373.00	
£7,235 x 40%	2,894.00	
£39,100 Income Tax Liability	9,267.00	
Less already paid	4,880.00	
Income tax to pay	4,387.00	

Note

The trading income is based on the accounting year to 31/12/14, because it ends in the tax year 2014/15.

The employment income is based on the amount received in the tax year, irrespective of the period that it relates to.

1.6 (a)   false

(b)   true

(c)   false

(d)   false

(e)   true

(f)   false

CHAPTER 2: INCOME FROM PROPERTY

2.1

		£
Rental Income for period 6/7/14 - 5/4/15	(£5,000 x 9/12)	3,750
Less		
Insurance (9 months at £25)		225
Repairs		200
Assessable property income for 2014/15		3,325

2.2

		£
Rental Income for period 6/11/14 - 5/4/15	(£400 x 5)	2,000
Less		
Mortgage Interest (5 months at £150)		750
Insurance (5 months at £30)		150
Agent's Fees (£1,200 x 5/12)		500
Assessable property income for 2014/15		600

The legal fees relating to the purchase of the property are a capital cost.

2.3

	£	£
Rental Income Receivable		10,000
less allowable expenditure:		
Council Tax	700	
Water Rates	300	
Insurance	400	
Managing Agent's Charges	1,000	
Wear & Tear Allowance		
(£10,000 – £700 – £300) x 10%	900	
		3,300
Assessable property income		6,700

2.4   (1)

	No 1	No 2	No 3	Total
	£	£	£	£
Rental Income	8,000	6,000	5,500	19,500
Less allowable expenditure:				
Council Tax	800	650	400	1,850
Loan Interest	3,600	2,000	4,000	9,600
Property Insurance	400	300	250	950
Redecoration	-	600	-	600
Repainting Windows	500	450	500	1,450
Other Repairs	300	400	200	900
Accountancy Fees	150	150	150	450
Wear & Tear Allowance	720	535	510	1,765
Profit / (Loss)	1,530	915	(510)	1,935
Less loss brought forward				1,000
Property Income				935

The council tax for property three is allowed since it relates to the period that it is occupied. Other expenses for this property relate to the period that it was owned for the business of letting and are therefore allowable.

(2)

Property income

Do not include furnished holiday lettings, Real Estate Investment Trust or Property Authorised Investment Funds dividends/distributions here.

20	Total rents and other income from property
	£ 19500 · 00

21	Tax taken off any income in box 20 - *read the notes*
	£ · 00

22	Premiums for the grant of a lease - from box E on the Working Sheet - *read the notes*
	£ · 00

23	Reverse premiums and inducements
	£ · 00

Property expenses

24	Rent, rates, insurance, ground rents etc.
	£ 2800 · 00

25	Property repairs and maintenance
	£ 2950 · 00

26	Loan interest and other financial costs
	£ 9600 · 00

27	Legal, management and other professional fees
	£ 450 · 00

28	Costs of services provided, including wages
	£ · 00

29	Other allowable property expenses
	£ · 00

Calculating your taxable profit or loss

30	Private use adjustment - *read the notes*
	£ · 00

31	Balancing charges - *read the notes*
	£ · 00

32	Annual Investment Allowance
	£ · 00

33	Business Premises Renovation Allowance (Assisted Areas only) - *read the notes*
	£ · 00

34	All other capital allowances
	£ · 00

35	Landlord's Energy Saving Allowance
	£ · 00

36	10% wear and tear allowance - *for furnished residential accommodation only*
	£ 1765 · 00

37	Rent a Room exempt amount
	£ · 00

38	Adjusted profit for the year - from box O on the Working Sheet - *read the notes*
	£ 1935 · 00

39	Loss brought forward used against this year's profits
	£ 1000 · 00

40	Taxable profit for the year (box 38 minus box 39)
	£ 935 · 00

41	Adjusted loss for the year - from box O on the Working Sheet - *read the notes*
	£ · 00

42	Loss set off against 2013-14 total income - *this will be unusual - read the notes*
	£ · 00

43	Loss to carry forward to following year, including unused losses brought forward
	£ · 00

2.5 1 Property Income Computation

	£	£
Rental Income Receivable		11,500
less allowable expenditure:		
Accountancy Fees	400	
Council Tax	650	
Water Rates	350	
Insurance	300	
Mortgage Interest	2,300	
Managing Agent's Charges	1,000	
Wear & Tear Allowance	1,050	
		6,050
Property Income		5,450

2 Income Tax Computation

	Income	Tax Paid
	£	£
Employment Income	41,500	6,300
Property Income	5,450	-
Total Income	46,950	6,300
Less Personal Allowance	10,000	
Taxable Income	36,950	

Income Tax Calculation:

31,865 x 20%		6,373.00
5,085 x 40%		2,034.00
36,950	Income Tax Liability	8,407.00
	Less Paid	6,300.00
	Income Tax to Pay	2,107.00

2.6

	Three bedroom house £	One bedroom flat £
Income	8,100	4,500
Expenses:		
Irrecoverable rent*	1,800	
Management charge	504	
Council tax and water		1,400
Insurance		270
Wear and tear		310
Profits	5,796	2,520

* Irrecoverable rent could alternatively be shown by reducing the income figure.

2.7 Statements (a), (d), (e) and (g) are true. The rest are false.

CHAPTER 3: INCOME FROM SAVINGS AND INVESTMENTS

3.1 **Savings Income:**

Details	Amount Rec'd	Tax Ded'd	Assessable Amount
Nat East Int	£1,600	£400	£2,000

Dividend Income:

Details	Amount Rec'd	Tax Credit	Assessable Amount
Osborne plc	£2,700	£300	£3,000

3.2 **Savings Income:**

Details	Amount Rec'd	Tax Ded'd	Assessable Amount
Oldport Int	£1,680	£420	£2,100
PCR Deb Int	£2,000	£500	£2,500
Exchequer Stock	£6,500	-	£6,500
	£10,180	£920	£11,100

Dividend Income:

Details	Amount Rec'd	Tax Credit	Assessable Amount
PCR plc div	£1,440	£160	£1,600

Note that the premium bond prize is exempt from income tax.

3.3 **Income Tax Computation**

	Income	Tax Paid
	£	£
Employment Income	28,500	3,700
Property Income	1,900	-
B/S Int	1,500	300
Dividends	4,000	400
Total Income	35,900	4,400
Less Personal Allowance	10,000	
Taxable Income	25,900	

Analysis of Taxable Income:

General Income	(£28,500 + £1,900 − £10,000)	£20,400
Savings Income		£1,500
Dividend Income		£4,000
		£25,900

	£	£
Income Tax Calculation:		
General Income:		
£20,400 x 20%	4,080.00	
		4,080.00
Savings Income:		
£1,500 x 20% (all in this band)	300.00	
		300.00
Dividend Income:		
£4,000 x 10% (all in this band)	400.00	
		400.00
Income Tax Liability		4,780.00
Less Paid		4,400.00
Income Tax to Pay		380.00

3.4 Income Tax Computation

	Income	Tax Paid
	£	£
Employment Income	21,600	2,320
Savings Income	2,000	400
Dividend Income	3,000	300
Total Income	26,600	3,020
Less Personal Allowance	10,000	
Taxable Income	16,600	

Analysis of Taxable Income:

General Income	(£21,600 – £10,000)	£11,600
Savings Income		£2,000
Dividend Income		£3,000
		£16,600

Income Tax Calculation:

General Income:

£11,600 x 20%	2,320.00	
		2,320.00

Savings Income:

£2,000 x 20% (all in this band)	400.00	
		400.00

Dividend Income:

£3,000 x 10% (all in this band)	300.00	
		300.00
Income Tax Liability		3,020.00
Less Paid		3,020.00
Income Tax to Pay		NIL

3.5 **(a)**

Savings Income

Date	Details	Amount Received	Tax Deducted	Assessable Amount
		£	£	£
30/6/14	3.5% War Loan	1,500.00	-	1,500.00
31/1/15	Bank of North'd	9,500.00	2,375.00	11,875.00
31/3/15	Osborne Bank	600.00	150.00	750.00
Total		11,600.00	2,525.00	14,125.00

Dividend Income

Date	Details	Amount Received	Tax Credit	Assessable Amount
		£	£	£
31/5/14	Growth plc	3,600.00	400.00	4,000.00

Note that the interest from the NISA is exempt, and that the receipts dated 31/3/14 and 30/6/15 fall outside the tax year 2014/15.

(b)

Income Tax Computation

	Income £	Tax paid £
Employment Income	5,000	0
Savings Income (as above)	14,125	2,525
Dividend Income (as above)	4,000	400
Total Income	23,125	2,925
Less Personal Allowance	10,000	
Taxable Income	13,125	

Analysis of Taxable Income:

General Income	(£5,000 – £10,000 = £–5,000)	£NIL
Savings Income	(£14,125 – £5,000)	£9,125
Dividend Income		£4,000
		£13,125

Note that the balance of the personal allowance is set against savings income.

Income Tax Calculation:

General Income – NIL

Savings Income:

£2,880 x 10%	288.00	
£6,245 x 20%	1,249.00	
£9,125		1,537.00

Dividend Income:

£4,000 x 10%	(all in this band)	400.00	
			400.00
	Income Tax Liability		1,937.00
	Less Paid		2,925.00
	Income Tax to be refunded		(988.00)

3.6

Received net	Received gross
Bank accounts	Government Securities (Gilts)
Building society accounts	
Loan stock from unquoted companies	

3.7

Cash NISAs and stocks and shares NISAs are subject to a maximum total investment in the tax year of £15,000	✔
Investment can be made in cash NISAs during the tax year with any number of providers	
Joint NISA accounts can be opened, but only by married couples	
NISAs can only be opened by individuals who are resident in the UK	✔
At the end of the tax year the tax-free status of investments made in a stocks and shares NISA expires	
The total invested in a stocks and shares NISA can subsequently be transferred to a cash NISA	✔

CHAPTER 4: INCOME FROM EMPLOYMENT

4.1

		£
Basic salary		18,000
Commission rec'd	30/4/14	1,200
	31/7/14	1,450
	31/10/14	1,080
	31/1/15	1,250
Employment income assessable amount 2014/15		22,980

4.2   Assessable   (b), (c), (e), (f), (g – home to work is private mileage)

   Tax-Free   (a), (d – interest rate higher than official rate), (h)

4.3

		£
Basic salary		20,000
Company car	(£11,500 x 17%)	1,955
Fuel for car	(£21,700 x 17%)	3,689
Credit card – private expenditure		100
(fuel covered by scale charge)		
Healthcare insurance		730
Employment income assessable amount		26,474

4.4

1			£
	Basic Salary		28,000
	Less 6% pension contribution		1,680
	Pay (per P60)		26,320
	Vouchers (cost to employer)		850
	Excess business mileage paid		
	10,000 x (60p – 45p)	1,500	
	1,500 x (60p – 25p)	525	
			2,025
	Hotel expenses received		250
			29,445
	Less allowable expenses:		
	Hotel costs	250	
	Professional fees	170	
			(420)
	Assessable amount		29,025

2   See tax form extracts on next page.

HM Revenue & Customs

Employment
Tax year 6 April 2013 to 5 April 2014

Your name

S U E   M E E

Your Unique Taxpayer Reference (UTR)

Complete an *Employment* page for each employment or directorship

1 Pay from this employment – the total from your P45 or P60 – *before tax was taken off*

£ 2 6 3 2 0 · 0 0

2 UK tax taken off pay in box 1

£ · 0 0

3 Tips and other payments not on your P60 – *read the Employment notes*

£ · 0 0

4 PAYE tax reference of your employer (on your P45/P60)

/

5 Your employer's name

C O N T R A X   &   C O

6 If you were a company director, put 'X' in the box

7 And, if the company was a close company, put 'X' in the box

8 If you are a part-time teacher in England or Wales and are on the Repayment of Teachers' Loans Scheme for this employment, put 'X' in the box

Benefits from your employment – use your form P11D (or equivalent information)

9 Company cars and vans – *the total 'cash equivalent' amount*

£ · 0 0

10 Fuel for company cars and vans – *the total 'cash equivalent' amount*

£ · 0 0

11 Private medical and dental insurance – *the total 'cash equivalent' amount*

£ · 0 0

12 Vouchers, credit cards and excess mileage allowance

£ 2 8 7 5 · 0 0

13 Goods and other assets provided by your employer – *the total value or amount*

£ · 0 0

14 Accommodation provided by your employer – *the total value or amount*

£ · 0 0

15 Other benefits (including interest-free and low interest loans) – *the total 'cash equivalent' amount*

£ · 0 0

16 Expenses payments received and balancing charges

£ 2 5 0 · 0 0

Employment expenses

17 Business travel and subsistence expenses

£ 2 5 0 · 0 0

18 Fixed deductions for expenses

£ · 0 0

19 Professional fees and subscriptions

£ 1 7 0 · 0 0

20 Other expenses and capital allowances

£ · 0 0

4.5

		£
1	Basic Salary	20,000
	Less 5% pension contribution	1,000
	Pay (per P60)	19,000
	Company car (1)	
	(£18,000 x 30% x 5/12)	2,250
	Company car (2)	
	((£20,000 – £1,000) x 21% x 7/12) 2,327	
		4,577
	Car fuel (car 2 only)	
	(£21,700 x 21% x 7/12)	2,658
	Dental treatment	500
	Employment Income	26,735

(Mortgage is not assessable since interest charged is over official rate)

2

	Rec'd	**Tax**	**Assessable**
Dividends	£1,800	£200	£2,000
Interest	£1,200	£300	£1,500

3 **Income tax computation**

	Income	**Tax paid**
	£	£
Employment Income	26,735	3,350
Interest	1,500	300
Dividends	2,000	200
	30,235	3,850
less personal allowance	10,000	
	20,235	

Analysis of income:

General	£16,735
Savings	£1,500
Dividends	£2,000
Total	£20,235

Tax:	£
On General Income:	
16,735 x 20%	3,347.00
On Savings Income	
1,500 x 20%	300.00
On Dividend Income	
2,000 x 10%	200.00
Tax liability	3,847.00
Less paid	3,850.00
Balance to be refunded	(3.00)

4.6

Contract of service is for:	Employment
Contract for services is for:	Self Employment
Choose work hours and charge for work done	Self Employment
No need to provide own equipment	Employment
Told how, when and where to do work	Employment
Can employ helper or substitute	Self Employment
Correct substandard work at own cost	Self Employment

4.7 **(1)** (£24,000 + £20,000)/2 x 7/12 x 0.25% = £32

(2) (c)

(3) Yes, Yes, No

(4) (a)

(5) (a) and (d) are correct

CHAPTER 5: PREPARING INCOME TAX COMPUTATIONS

5.1 **(a)** Gross equivalent amounts:

Gift Aid £2,000 x 100/80 = £2,500

Pension £3,040 x 100/80 = £3,800

(b)   Jo will get tax relief at her highest rate (40%) on her gross payments (20% when the payments are made and the other 20% in calculating her tax). The cost of her payments after tax relief will therefore be:

Gift Aid £2,500 less 40% = £1,500.

Pension £3,800 less 40% = £2,280.

5.2   (a)   **Income Tax Computation**

	£	£ Tax Paid
Property Income	9,400	-
Employment Income	26,500	3,300
Interest rec'd	5,000	1,000
Dividend income	12,000	1,200
Total Income	52,900	5,500
Less Personal Allowance	10,000	
Taxable Income	42,900	

Analysis of Taxable Income:

General Income (£9,400 + £26,500 – £10,000)	£25,900
Savings Income	£5,000
Dividend Income	£12,000
	£42,900

The basic rate band will be increased by the gross equivalent of the pension payment (£2,400 x 100/80 = £3,000). This makes the new top of the band £31,865 + £3,000 = £34,865.

Income Tax Calculation:

General Income:	£	£
£25,900 x 20%	5,180.00	
		5,180.00
Savings Income		
£5,000 x 20% (all in this band)		1,000.00
Dividend Income		
£3,965 x 10% (to £34,865 cumulative)	396.50	
£8,035 x 32.5%	2,611.37	
		3,007.87
Income tax liability		9,187.87
Less paid		5,500.00
Balance to pay		3,687.87

(b)   Payments will need to be made on account for 2015/16 (unless a claim is made that 2015/16 tax will be lower).

Each payment on account will be 50% of £3,687.87 = £1,843 (rounded down), payable on 31/1/16 (along with the 2014/15 balance) and 31/7/16.

5.3 Penalty for late submission of return	£100
Penalty for being over 30 days late with final payment 5% of tax amount of £400 (not time-apportioned)	£20
Interest on tax (for two months) 3% x £400 x 2/12	£2
	£122

5.4

(a)

	£
Rent received	6,300
less insurance	350
less wear & tear	630
	5,320
less loss b/f	250
Property income	5,070

(b)

	£
Salary	148,500
Excess mileage allowance paid 2,000 miles x (80p – 45p)	700
Less ACCA membership fee	(205)
Employment Income	148,995

(c)   Savings and Dividend Income

	Amount Rec'd £	Tax £	Assessable £
Bank Interest	800	200	1,000
Dividends	1,260	140	1,400

(d)   Income Tax Computation

	£	£ Tax Paid
Property Income	5,070	nil
Employment Income	148,995	48,220
Savings and Investment Income:		
(interest rec'd)	1,000	200
(dividend income)	1,400	140
Total Income	156,465	48,560
Less Personal Allowance (eliminated)	0	
Taxable Income	156,465	

Analysis of Taxable Income:	
General Income (£5,070 + £148,995)	154,065
Savings Income	1,000
Dividend Income	1,400
	156,465

Income Tax Calculation:

General Income	£	£
£31,865 x 20%		6,373.00
£118,135 x 40%		47,254.00
£4,065 x 45%		1,829.25
£154,065		£55,456.25
Savings Income		
£1,000 x 45% (all in this band)		450.00
Dividend Income £1,400 x 37.5% (all in this band)		525.00
Income tax liability		56,431.25
Less paid		48,560.00
Balance to pay		7,871.25

(e)   The balance must be paid by 31/1/16, and the paper-based return must be submitted by 31/10/15.

5.5

	£
Income	26,000
Gross dividends	1,040
	27,040
Personal allowance	10,480
Taxable income	16,560
General Income	
(£26,000 – £10,480) x 20%	3,104
Dividend Income	
£1,040 x 10%	104
Tax Liability	3,208

Workings:

Personal Allowance: £10,500 – 50% x (27,040 – £27,000) = £10,480

5.6   Half of the tax liability for any year is paid by 31 January in that tax year, and the other half is paid by 31 July following the tax year. This is based on an estimate, using the preceding tax years' liability. Therefore, when your father paid his tax liability on 31 January 2014 and 31 July 2014 for 2013/14, this would have been an estimate based on his liability for the year before.

When the final figures were sent to HMRC, they worked out that these two instalments were not enough to cover the full liability; hence the £1,400 is the balance of tax due.

As explained, the instalment on 31 January 2015 for this current tax year is based on the actual liability for the previous year, 2013/14. If the instalments he pays exceed his actual liability (i.e. he overpays for 2014/15), he will receive a refund from HMRC.

However, he can claim to reduce these instalments if he knows that his income will not be as high as it was last year. Whilst this is fine, your father needs to be careful. If he makes an incorrect claim to reduce these instalments, HMRC will charge him interest on the difference between the instalments that should have been paid and what was actually paid.

5.7

	£
Employment Income	89,000
Gross dividends	20,000
	109,000
Personal allowance	7,000
Taxable income	102,000
General Income	
(£31,865 + £3,000) x 20%	6,973
(£82,000* – £34,865) x 40%	18,854
Dividend Income	
£20,000 x 32.5%	6,500
Tax Liability	32,327

Workings:

Adjusted net income: £89,000 + £20,000 - £3,000 = £106,000

Personal Allowance: £10,000 – 50% x (£106,000 – £100,000)= £7,000

* General income: £89,000 – £7,000 = £82,000

CHAPTER 6: CAPITAL GAINS TAX – THE MAIN PRINCIPLES

6.1   Chargeable Assets: (a), (b), (c).
Exempt Assets: (d), (e – wasting chattel), (f – chattel sold for a gain for under £6,000), (g), (h).

6.2

	£	£
Gain	15,000	
less annual exempt amount	(11,000)	
Amount subject to CGT	4,000	
Capital Gains Tax:		
£4,000 x 18% (all within basic rate band)		720.00

6.3

	£	£
Capital Gain	35,000	
Less Capital Loss	(9,000)	
Net Gain	26,000	
less annual exempt amount	(11,000)	
Amount subject to CGT	15,000	
Capital Gains Tax:		
£3,865 x 18% (£31,865 – £28,000)		695.70
£11,135 x 28%		3,117.80
		3,813.50

6.4

	£
Proceeds	130,000
less Cost	(60,000)
Gain	70,000

	£
Gain	70,000
less Annual exempt amount	(11,000)
Subject to CGT	59,000

	£
Capital Gains Tax (all at 28%)	16,520.00

6.5   **Flat**

	£
Proceeds	165,000
less Cost	(50,000)
Gain	115,000

Shares

Proceeds	32,000
less Cost	(52,000)
Loss	(20,000)
Gain on flat	115,000
Loss on shares	(20,000)
Net Gain	95,000
less Annual exempt amount	(11,000)
Subject to CGT	84,000
Capital Gains Tax	
£84,000 x 28%	23,520.00

6.6 Ivan Asset

(a)

Shares in Astro plc

	£
Proceeds (5,000 x £12.00)	60,000
less cost (5,000 x £8.00)	(40,000)
Gain	20,000

Morgan Car – Exempt Asset

Antique dresser

	£
Proceeds	14,000
less cost	(9,000)
Gain	5,000

Shares in Expo Ltd

	£
Market Value (4,000 x £5.00)	20,000
less cost (4,000 x £2.00)	(8,000)
Gain	12,000

(b)

The gains can now be added together, and the loss offset.

	£
Gains:	
Astro plc shares	20,000
Antique dresser	5,000
Expo Ltd shares	12,000
	37,000
less loss brought forward	(15,000)
	22,000
less annual exempt amount	(11,000)
Taxable amount	11,000
Capital gains tax £11,000 x 28%	3,080.00

6.7 Justin Shaw

(a)

Yacht – Exempt as a wasting chattel

Shares in Captain plc

	£
Proceeds (1,000 x £15.00)	15,000
less cost (1,000 x £9.00)	(9,000)
Gain	6,000

Antique painting

	£
Proceeds	14,000
less cost	(10,000)
Gain	4,000

Shares in Boater Ltd

	£
Market Value (3,000 x £7.00)	21,000
less cost (3,000 x £3.00)	(9,000)
Gain	12,000

(b)

	£
Gains:	
Captain plc shares	6,000
Antique painting	4,000
Boater Ltd shares	12,000
	22,000
less loss brought forward*	(11,000)
Balance	11,000
less annual exempt amount	(11,000)
Taxable amount	0

There is no CGT liability.

*Of the £18,000 loss brought forward, only £11,000 is used so that a balance of £11,000 is left (the amount of the annual exemption). This leaves a loss of £7,000 to be carried forward to the next year.

6.8 **(1)** Deemed proceeds used
     (2) No gain or loss basis
     (3) Actual proceeds used
     (4) Deemed proceeds used
     (5) No gain or loss basis

6.9 **(1)** (b)
     (2) False

6.10 **(1)** False
     (2) True
     (3) False

CHAPTER 7: CAPITAL GAINS TAX – SOME SPECIAL RULES

7.1

	£
Land	
Proceeds	30,000
less apportioned cost:	
£50,000 x £30,000 / £150,000	(10,000)
Gain	20,000

Cottage

Proceeds	300,000
less cost	(60,000)
extension	(50,000)
Gain	190,000

Total gains: Land	20,000
Cottage	190,000
Total gains	210,000
less annual exempt amount	(11,000)
Amount subject to CGT	199,000

Capital Gains Tax:

£199,000 x 28% = £55,720.00

7.2

	£
Painting	
Proceeds	20,000
less cost	(5,000)
less restoration	(6,000)
Gain	9,000

Table	
Proceeds	7,800
less costs: (£1,400 + £100)	(1,500)
Provisional Gain	6,300

But gain limited to 5/3 (£7,800 − £6,000) = £3,000.

	£
Total gains: Painting	9,000
Table	3,000
	12,000
less annual exempt amount	(11,000)
Amount subject to CGT	1,000

Capital Gains Tax:

£1,000 x 18% = £180.00 (all in basic rate band)

7.3

Necklace	£
Deemed Proceeds (market value)	8,000
less cost:	(5,000)
Gain	3,000

Gain limited to 5/3 (£8,000 – £6,000) = £3,333 – limit does not apply.

Car is an exempt asset

House is not entirely exempt:

World holiday period counts as deemed occupation under the 'absence for any reason' rule since it is for less than 3 years and is between periods of actual occupation.

1½ of the final six years of absence counts as deemed occupation since it was a PPR before this. The house is therefore exempt for 22.5 years of the 27 years ownership, and chargeable for 4.5 years.

	£
Proceeds	470,000
less cost	(80,000)
Gain	390,000
Exempt £390,000 x 22.5/27	325,000
Chargeable £390,000 x 4.5/27	65,000
Gains Summary:	
Necklace	3,000
House	65,000
Total Gains	68,000
less exempt amount	(11,000)
Taxable	57,000
Capital Gains Tax	
£1,865 x 18% =	335.70
£55,135 x 28% =	15,437.80
	15,773.50

7.4 The 3,000 rights issue shares (1 for 5 of the total holding of 15,000 shares) acquired in January 2000 will be linked with the original shares from which the rights derive. Therefore the shares will be added into the pool.

The disposal of 14,400 shares in July 2014 will therefore be matched entirely with the shares that are in the pool:

Pool Working:

		Number	Cost £
1/1/1992	Purchase	3,000	9,000
1/1/1999	Purchase	12,000	42,000
		15,000	51,000
1/1/2000	Rights Issue (1 for 5)	3,000	6,000
		18,000	57,000
30/7/2014	Disposal	(14,400)	(45,600)
	Pool balance after disposal	3,600	11,400

Share disposal July 2014	£
Proceeds	72,000
less cost	(45,600)
Gain	26,400

Dresser disposal	
Proceeds	6,900
less cost	(3,000)
Gain	3,900

But gain limited to 5/3 (£6,900 − £6,000) = £1,500.

		£
Total gains: Shares		26,400
Dresser		1,500
Total gains		27,900
less annual exempt amount		(11,000)
Amount subject to CGT		16,900

Capital Gains Tax

£16,900 x 28%	4,732.00

7.5 **1** The 2,000 shares sold on 15/11/2001 would have been matched against:
- the 1,800 shares bought on 1/12/2001, and
- 200 shares from the FA 1985 pool

2 The 2,500 shares sold on 15/7/2014 will be matched against the shares in the FA 1985 pool.

3 *Pool Working:*

		Number	Cost £
1/5/1985	Purchase	1,000	8,000
1/1/1992	Purchase	1,750	15,750
1/1/1995	Purchase	1,500	10,650
		4,250	34,400
15/11/2001	Part Disposal	(200)	(1,619)
		4,050	32,781
15/7/2014	Disposal	(2,500)	(20,235)
	Pool balance	1,550	12,546

Disposal of Shares:

Proceeds (2,500 x £12)	30,000	
less cost	(20,235)	as above
Gain	9,765	

4 Computations on other asset disposals:

Land

	£
Proceeds	20,000
less apportioned cost:	
£5,000 x £20,000 / £100,000	(1,000)
Gain	19,000

Antique Brooch

	£
Proceeds	9,600
less cost	(5,500)
Provisional gain	4,100

Gain is limited to 5/3 (£9,600 – £6,000) = £6,000 – limit does not apply.

Antique table

	£
Proceeds	12,000
less cost	(13,500)
Loss	(1,500)

5

	£
Gains:	
Shares	9,765
Land	19,000
Antique brooch	4,100
	32,865
less loss on antique table	(1,500)
Net gains	31,365
less annual exempt amount	(11,000)
Amount subject to CGT	20,365

Capital Gains Tax:
£20,365 x 28% = £5,702.20

6   Tax form completed as follows.

HM Revenue & Customs

Capital gains summary
Tax year 6 April 2013 to 5 April 2014

1 Your name

E D W A R D

2 Your Unique Taxpayer Reference (UTR)

Summary of your enclosed computations

Please read the *Capital gains summary notes* before filling in this section. **You must enclose your computations, including details of each gain or loss, as well as filling in the boxes.**

ℹ To get notes and helpsheets that will help you fill in this form, go to hmrc.gov.uk/selfassessmentforms

3 Total gains *(Boxes 21 + 27 + 33 + 34)*

£ 3 2 8 6 5 · 0 0

4 Gains qualifying for Entrepreneurs' Relief (but excluding gains deferred from before 23 June 2010) - *read the notes*

£ · 0 0

5 Gains invested under Seed Enterprise Investment Scheme and qualifying for exemption - *read the notes*

£ · 0 0

6 Total losses of the year - *enter '0' if there are none*

£ 1 5 0 0 · 0 0

7 Losses brought forward and used in the year

£ · 0 0

8 Adjustment to Capital Gains Tax - *read the notes*

£ ▬ · 0 0

9 Additional liability for non-resident or dual resident trusts

£ · 0 0

10 Losses available to be carried forward to later years

£ · 0 0

11 Losses used against an earlier year's gain (special circumstances apply - *read the notes*)

£ · 0 0

12 Losses used against income – amount claimed against 2013–14 income - *read the notes*

£ · 0 0

13 Amount in box 12 relating to shares to which Enterprise Investment Scheme/Seed Enterprise Investment Scheme relief is attributable

£ · 0 0

14 Losses used against income – amount claimed against 2012–13 income - *read the notes*

£ · 0 0

15 Amount in box 14 relating to shares to which Enterprise Investment Scheme/Seed Enterprise Investment Scheme relief is attributable

£ · 0 0

16 Income losses of 2013–14 set against gains

£ · 0 0

17 Deferred gains from before 23 June 2010 qualifying for Entrepreneurs' Relief

£ · 0 0

Listed shares and securities

18 Number of disposals - *read the notes*

`1`

19 Disposal proceeds

£ `3 0 0 0 0 · 0 0`

20 Allowable costs (including purchase price)

£ `2 0 2 3 5 · 0 0`

21 Gains in the year, before losses

£ `9 7 6 5 · 0 0`

22 If you are making any claim or election, put 'X' in the box

23 If your computations include any estimates or valuations, put 'X' in the box

Unlisted shares and securities

24 Number of disposals - *read the notes*

25 Disposal proceeds

£ `· 0 0`

26 Allowable costs (including purchase price)

£ `· 0 0`

27 Gains in the year, before losses

£ `· 0 0`

28 If you are making any claim or election, put 'X' in the box

29 If your computations include any estimates or valuations, put 'X' in the box

Property and other assets and gains

30 Number of disposals

`3`

31 Disposal proceeds

£ `4 1 6 0 0 · 0 0`

32 Allowable costs (including purchase price)

£ `2 0 0 0 0 · 0 0`

33 Gains in the year, before losses

£ `2 3 1 0 0 · 0 0`

34 Attributed gains where personal losses cannot be set off

£ `· 0 0`

35 If you are making any claim or election, put 'X' in the box

36 If your computations include any estimates or valuations, put 'X' in the box

Any other information

37 Please give any other information in this space

7.6

(a)

Occupation / Deemed Occupation	Non-occupation
1/2/2000 - 31/1/2005	1/2/2005 – 31/12/2012
1/1/2013 - 1/7/2014	

(b)

Total gain calculation: £

      Proceeds   205,000

      Cost   70,000

      Total gain   135,000

Chargeable gain   £135,000 x $\dfrac{\text{non-occupation period}}{\text{total ownership period}}$

         =   £135,000 x $\dfrac{\text{95 months}}{\text{173 months}}$

         =   £74,132

7.7

Asset	Sale proceeds	Cost	Statement
1	£4,000	£3,000	Exempt asset
2	£12,000	£8,000	Calculate gain as normal
3	£7,000	£5,000	Chattel marginal relief applies
4	£3,000	£8,000	Sale proceeds to be £6,000
5	£15,000	£21,000	Calculate loss as normal

Appendix

These pages may be photocopied for student use.

It is recommended that they are enlarged to A4 size.

These pages are also available for download from the Resources Section of www.osbornebooks.co.uk or from www.hmrc.gov.uk

The tax forms include:

Note that all these forms relate to the tax year 2013/14 as the 2014/15 versions were not available when this book was published.

HM Revenue & Customs

Tax Return 2014
Tax year 6 April 2013 to 5 April 2014

UTR
NINO
Employer reference

Date

HM Revenue & Customs office address

┌   ┐

└   ┘

Telephone

Issue address

┌   ┐

└   ┘

For
Reference

Your tax return

This notice requires you, by law, to make a return of your taxable income and capital gains, and any documents requested, for the year from 6 April 2013 to 5 April 2014.

Deadlines

We must receive your tax return by these dates:
- if you are using a **paper** return – by **31 October 2014** (or 3 months after the date of this notice if that's later), or
- if you are filing a return **online** – by **31 January 2015** (or 3 months after the date of this notice if that's later).

If your **return** is late you will be charged a **£100 penalty**. If your return is more than 3 months late, you will be charged daily penalties of £10 a day.

If you **pay** late you will be charged interest and a late payment penalty.

How to file your return

Most people file online. To do this go to **hmrc.gov.uk/online** To file on paper, please fill in this form using the rules below.

Use black ink and capital letters

Cross out any mistakes and write the correct information below

4 Name of bank or building society
ANY BANK

8 State Pension lump sum
£ 2 4 3 5 0 . 0 0
4 9

9 Tax taken off box 8
£ 4 7 0 1 . 0 0

Please round up tax paid, for example, £4,700.21 would be £4701

10 Pensions (other than State Pension), retirem

- Enter your figures to the nearest pound – ignore the pence. Round down income and round up expenses and tax paid – it is to your benefit.
- If a box does not apply, please leave it blank – do not strike through empty boxes or write anything else.

Starting your tax return

Before you start to fill it in, look through your tax return to make sure there is a section for all your income and claims – you may need some separate supplementary pages (see page TR 2 and the Tax Return Guide). To get notes and helpsheets that will help you fill in this form, go to **hmrc.gov.uk/selfassessmentforms**

Your personal details

1 Your date of birth – *it helps get your tax right*
DD MM YYYY

2 Your name and address – *if it is different from what is on the front of this form. Please write the correct details underneath the wrong ones, and put 'X' in the box*

3 Your phone number

4 Your National Insurance number – *leave blank if the correct number is shown above*

What makes up your tax return

To make a **complete** return of your taxable income and gains for the year to 5 April 2014 you may need to complete some **separate supplementary pages**. Answer the following questions by putting 'X' in the 'Yes' or 'No' box.

1 Employment

If you were an employee, director, office holder or agency worker in the year to 5 April 2014, do you need to complete *Employment* pages? Please read the guide before answering.

Fill in a separate *Employment* page for each employment, directorship, etc. On each *Employment* page you complete, enter any other payments, expenses or benefits related to that employment. Say how many *Employment* pages you are completing in the *Number* box below.

Yes ☐   No ☐   Number ☐

2 Self-employment

Did you work for yourself (on your 'own account' or in self-employment) in the year to 5 April 2014? (Answer 'Yes' if you were a 'Name' at Lloyd's.)

Fill in a separate *Self-employment* page for each business. On each *Self-employment* page you complete, enter any payments or expenses related to that business. Say how many businesses you had in the *Number* box below.

Yes ☐   No ☐   Number ☐

3 Partnership

Were you in partnership? Fill in a separate *Partnership* page for each partnership you were a partner in and say how many partnerships you had in the *Number* box below.

Yes ☐   No ☐   Number ☐

4 UK property

Did you receive any income from UK property (including rents and other UK income from land you own or lease out)? *Read the guide if you have furnished holiday lettings.*

Yes ☐   No ☐

5 Foreign

If you:
• were entitled to any foreign income, or income gains
• have, or could have, received (directly or indirectly) income, or a capital payment or benefit from a person abroad as a result of any transfer of assets
• want to claim relief for foreign tax paid
read the guide to decide if you have to fill in the *Foreign* pages. Do you need to fill in the *Foreign* pages?

Yes ☐   No ☐

6 Trusts etc.

Did you receive, or are you treated as having received, income from a trust, settlement or the residue of a deceased person's estate? This does not include cash lump sums/transfer of assets, otherwise known as capital distributions, received under a will.

Yes ☐   No ☐

7 Capital gains summary

If you sold or disposed of any assets (including, for example, stocks, shares, land and property, a business), or had any chargeable gains, read the guide to decide if you have to fill in the *Capital gains summary* page. If you do, you must also provide separate computations.

Do you need to fill in the *Capital gains summary* page **and** provide computations?

Yes ☐   No ☐   Computation(s) provided ☐

8 Residence, remittance basis etc.

Were you, for all or part of the year to 5 April 2014, one or more of the following – not resident or not domiciled in the UK and claiming the remittance basis or dual resident in the UK and another country?

Yes ☐   No ☐

9 Supplementary pages

If you answered 'Yes' to any of questions 1 to 8, please check to see if **within this return**, there is a page dealing with that kind of income etc. If there is not, you will need separate supplementary pages. Do you need to get and fill in separate supplementary pages?

Yes ☐   No ☐

If 'Yes', you can go to hmrc.gov.uk/selfassessmentforms to download them, or phone **0300 200 3610** and ask us for the relevant pages.

*Some less common kinds of income and tax reliefs (not covered by questions 1 to 8), and details of disclosed tax avoidance schemes, should be returned on the **Additional information** pages enclosed in the tax return pack. Do you need to fill in the **Additional information** pages?*

Yes ☐   No ☐

Income

Interest and dividends from UK banks, building societies etc.

1 **Taxed UK interest etc.** - *the net amount after tax has been taken off. Read the guide*

£ [   ] • 0 0

2 **Untaxed UK interest etc.** - *amounts which have not had tax taken off. Read the guide*

£ [   ] • 0 0

3 **Dividends from UK companies** - *do not include the tax credit. Read the guide*

£ [   ] • 0 0

4 **Other dividends** - *do not include the tax credit. Read the guide*

£ [   ] • 0 0

5 **Foreign dividends (up to £300)** - *the amount in sterling after foreign tax was taken off. Do not include this amount in the Foreign pages*

£ [   ] • 0 0

6 **Tax taken off foreign dividends** - *the sterling equivalent*

£ [   ] • 0 0

UK pensions, annuities and other state benefits received

7 **State Pension** - *the gross amount shown on your pension statement. Read the guide*

£ [   ] • 0 0

8 **State Pension lump sum**

£ [   ] • 0 0

9 **Tax taken off box 8**

£ [   ] • 0 0

10 **Pensions (other than State Pension), retirement annuities and taxable triviality payments** - *give details of the payers, amounts paid and tax deducted in the 'Any other information' box, box 19, on page TR 7 - enter tax taken off in box 11*

£ [   ] • 0 0

11 **Tax taken off box 10**

£ [   ] • 0 0

12 **Taxable Incapacity Benefit and contribution-based Employment and Support Allowance** - *Read the guide*

£ [   ] • 0 0

13 **Tax taken off Incapacity Benefit in box 12**

£ [   ] • 0 0

14 **Jobseeker's Allowance**

£ [   ] • 0 0

15 **Total of any other taxable State Pensions and benefits**

£ [   ] • 0 0

Other UK income not included on supplementary pages

Do not use this section for income that should be returned on supplementary pages. Share schemes, gilts, stock dividends, life insurance gains and certain other kinds of income go on the *Additional information* pages in the tax return pack.

16 **Other taxable income** - *before expenses and tax taken off*

£ [   ] • 0 0

17 **Total amount of allowable expenses** - *Read the guide*

£ [   ] • 0 0

18 **Any tax taken off box 16**

£ [   ] • 0 0

19 **Benefit from pre-owned assets** - *Read the guide*

£ [   ] • 0 0

20 **Description of income in boxes 16 and 19** - *if there is not enough space here please give details in the 'Any other information' box, box 19, on page TR 7*

[   ]
[   ]
[   ]

Tax reliefs

Paying into registered pension schemes and overseas pension schemes

Do not include payments you make to your employer's pension scheme which are deducted from your pay before tax or payments made by your employer. If you paid in excess of £50,000, you should consider completing the 'Pension savings tax charges' section on page Ai 4 of the *Additional information* pages.

1 Payments to registered pension schemes where basic rate tax relief will be claimed by your pension provider (called 'relief at source'). Enter the payments and basic rate tax

£ · 0 0

2 Payments to a retirement annuity contract where basic rate tax relief will not be claimed by your provider

£ · 0 0

3 Payments to your employer's scheme which were not deducted from your pay before tax

£ · 0 0

4 Payments to an overseas pension scheme, which is not UK-registered, which are eligible for tax relief and were not deducted from your pay before tax

£ · 0 0

Charitable giving

5 Gift Aid payments made in the year to 5 April 2014

£ · 0 0

6 Total of any 'one-off' payments in box 5

£ · 0 0

7 Gift Aid payments made in the year to 5 April 2014 but treated as if made in the year to 5 April 2013

£ · 0 0

8 Gift Aid payments made after 5 April 2014 but to be treated as if made in the year to 5 April 2014

£ · 0 0

9 Value of qualifying shares or securities gifted to charity

£ · 0 0

10 Value of qualifying land and buildings gifted to charity

£ · 0 0

11 Value of qualifying investments gifted to non-UK charities in boxes 9 and 10

£ · 0 0

12 Gift Aid payments to non-UK charities in box 5

£ · 0 0

Blind Person's Allowance

13 If you are registered blind on a local authority or other register, put 'X' in the box

14 Enter the name of the local authority or other register

15 If you want your spouse's, or civil partner's, surplus allowance, put 'X' in the box

16 If you want your spouse, or civil partner, to have your surplus allowance, put 'X' in the box

Other less common reliefs are on the *Additional information* pages enclosed in the tax return pack.

Student Loan repayments

Please read the guide before filling in boxes 1 to 3.

1 If you have received notification from the Student Loans Company that repayment of an Income Contingent Student Loan began before 6 April 2014, put 'X' in the box

3 If you think your loan may be fully repaid within the next two years, put 'X' in the box

2 If your employer has deducted Student Loan repayments enter the amount deducted

£ [   ] · 0 0

High Income Child Benefit Charge

Only fill in this section if:
- your income was over £50,000, **and**
- you or your partner (if you have one) were entitled to receive Child Benefit (this also applies if someone else claims Child Benefit for a child who lives with you and pays you or your partner for the child's upkeep), **and**
- **couples only** – your income was higher than your partner's.

Please read the guide.

If you have to pay this charge for the 2014-15 tax year and you do not want us to use your 2014-15 PAYE tax code to collect that tax during the year, put 'X' in box 3 on page TR 6.

1 Enter the total amount of Child Benefit you and your partner were entitled to receive for the year to 5 April 2014

£ [   ] · 0 0

2 Enter the number of children you and your partner were entitled to receive Child Benefit for on 5 April 2014

[   ]

Service companies

1 If you provided your services through a service company (a company which provides your personal services to third parties), enter the total of the dividends (including the tax credit) and salary (before tax was taken off) you withdrew from the company in the tax year - *Read the guide*

£ [   ] · 0 0

Finishing your tax return

ℹ️ **Calculating your tax** - if we receive your tax return by post or online by 31 October 2014, we will do the calculation for you and tell you how much you have to pay (or what your repayment will be) before 31 January 2015.

We will add the amount due to your Self Assessment Statement, together with any other amounts due.
Do not enter payments on account, or other payments you have made towards the amounts due, on your tax return. We will deduct these on your Self Assessment Statement.

If you want to calculate your tax, ask us for the *Tax calculation summary* pages and *notes*. The *notes* will help you work out any tax due or repayable, and if payments on account are necessary.

Tax refunded or set off

1 If you have had any 2013-14 Income Tax refunded or set off by us or Jobcentre Plus, enter the amount

£ [   ] · 0 0

If you have not paid enough tax

Use the payslip at the foot of your next statement (or reminder) from us to pay any tax due.

2	If you owe tax for 2013–14 and have a PAYE tax code, we will try to collect the tax due (if less than £3,000) through your tax code for 2015–16, unless you put 'X' in the box - *Read the guide*	3	If for 2014–15, you are likely to owe tax on the High Income Child Benefit Charge or on income other than employed earnings or pensions, and you do not want us to use your 2014–15 PAYE tax code to collect that tax during the year, put 'X' in the box - *Read the guide*

If you have paid too much tax

If you fill in your bank or building society account details we can make any repayment due straight into your account. This is the safest and quickest method. But, if you do not have a suitable account, put 'X' in box 9 and we will send you or your nominee a cheque.

4 **Name of bank or building society**

5 **Name of account holder (or nominee)**

6 **Branch sort code**

7 **Account number**

8 **Building society reference number**

9 **If you do not have a bank or building society account, or if you want us to send a cheque to you or to your nominee, put 'X' in the box**

10 **If you have entered a nominee's name in box 5, put 'X' in the box**

11 **If your nominee is your tax adviser, put 'X' in the box**

12 **Nominee's address**

13 **and postcode**

14 **To authorise your nominee to receive any repayment, you must sign in the box. A photocopy of your signature will not do**

9.6

Your tax adviser, if you have one

This section is optional. Please read the guide about authorising your tax adviser.

15 **Your tax adviser's name**

17 **The first line of their address including the postcode**

Postcode

16 **Their phone number**

18 **The reference your adviser uses for you**

Any other information

19 **Please give any other information in this space**

Signing your form and sending it back

Please fill in this section and sign and date the declaration at box 22.

20 **If this tax return contains provisional or estimated figures, put 'X' in the box**

21 **If you are enclosing separate supplementary pages, put 'X' in the box**

22 **Declaration**

I declare that the information I have given on this tax return and any supplementary pages is correct and complete to the best of my knowledge and belief.

I understand that I may have to pay financial penalties and face prosecution if I give false information.

Signature

Date *DD MM YYYY*

23 **If you have signed on behalf of someone else, enter the capacity. For example, executor, receiver**

24 **Enter the name of the person you have signed for**

25 **If you filled in boxes 23 and 24 enter your name**

26 **and your address**

Postcode

HM Revenue & Customs

Employment
Tax year 6 April 2013 to 5 April 2014

Your name

Your Unique Taxpayer Reference (UTR)

Complete an *Employment* page for each employment or directorship

1 Pay from this employment – the total from your P45 or P60 - *before tax was taken off*

£ · 0 0

2 UK tax taken off pay in box 1

£ · 0 0

3 Tips and other payments not on your P60
- *read the Employment notes*

£ · 0 0

4 PAYE tax reference of your employer (on your P45/P60)

/

5 Your employer's name

6 If you were a company director, put 'X' in the box

7 And, if the company was a close company, put 'X' in the box

8 If you are a part-time teacher in England or Wales and are on the Repayment of Teachers' Loans Scheme for this employment, put 'X' in the box

Benefits from your employment - use your form P11D (or equivalent information)

9 Company cars and vans
- *the total 'cash equivalent' amount*

£ · 0 0

10 Fuel for company cars and vans
- *the total 'cash equivalent' amount*

£ · 0 0

11 Private medical and dental insurance
- *the total 'cash equivalent' amount*

£ · 0 0

12 Vouchers, credit cards and excess mileage allowance

£ · 0 0

13 Goods and other assets provided by your employer
- *the total value or amount*

£ · 0 0

14 Accommodation provided by your employer
- *the total value or amount*

£ · 0 0

15 Other benefits (including interest-free and low interest loans) - *the total 'cash equivalent' amount*

£ · 0 0

16 Expenses payments received and balancing charges

£ · 0 0

Employment expenses

17 Business travel and subsistence expenses

£ · 0 0

18 Fixed deductions for expenses

£ · 0 0

19 Professional fees and subscriptions

£ · 0 0

20 Other expenses and capital allowances

£ · 0 0

Share schemes, employment lump sums, compensation, deductions and Seafarers' Earnings Deduction are on the *Additional information* pages enclosed in the tax return pack.

ⓘ **Share schemes, employment lump sums, compensation, deductions and Seafarers' Earnings Deduction** are on the *Additional information* pages enclosed in the tax return pack.

Second employment

Complete an *Employment* page for each employment or directorship

1 Pay from this employment – the total from your P45 or P60 – *before tax was taken off*

£ [   ] . 0 0

2 UK tax taken off pay in box 1

£ [   ] . 0 0

3 Tips and other payments not on your P60
– *read the Employment notes*

£ [   ] . 0 0

4 PAYE tax reference of your employer (on your P45/P60)

[   ] / [   ]

5 Your employer's name

[   ]

6 If you were a company director, put 'X' in the box

[ ]

7 And, if the company was a close company, put 'X' in the box

[ ]

8 If you are a part-time teacher in England or Wales and are on the Repayment of Teachers' Loans Scheme for this employment, put 'X' in the box

[ ]

Benefits from your employment – use your form P11D (or equivalent information)

9 Company cars and vans – the total 'cash equivalent' amount

£ [   ] . 0 0

10 Fuel for company cars and vans – the total 'cash equivalent' amount

£ [   ] . 0 0

11 Private medical and dental insurance – the total 'cash equivalent' amount

£ [   ] . 0 0

12 Vouchers, credit cards and excess mileage allowance

£ [   ] . 0 0

13 Goods and other assets provided by your employer – the total value or amount

£ [   ] . 0 0

14 Accommodation provided by your employer – the total value or amount

£ [   ] . 0 0

15 Other benefits (including interest-free and low interest loans) – the total 'cash equivalent' amount

£ [   ] . 0 0

16 Expenses payments received and balancing charges

£ [   ] . 0 0

Employment expenses

17 Business travel and subsistence expenses

£ [   ] . 0 0

18 Fixed deductions for expenses

£ [   ] . 0 0

19 Professional fees and subscriptions

£ [   ] . 0 0

20 Other expenses and capital allowances

£ [   ] . 0 0

ⓘ To get notes and helpsheets that will help you fill in this form, go to hmrc.gov.uk/selfassessmentforms

UK property

Tax year 6 April 2013 to 5 April 2014

HM Revenue & Customs

Your name	Your Unique Taxpayer Reference (UTR)

ℹ To get notes and helpsheets that will help you fill in this form, go to hmrc.gov.uk/selfassessmentforms

UK property details

1 Number of properties rented out

2 If all property income ceased in 2013–14 and you do not expect to receive such income in 2014–15, put 'X' in the box and consider if you need to fill in the *Capital gains summary* page

3 If you have any income from property let jointly, put 'X' in the box

4 If you are claiming Rent a Room relief and your rents are £4,250 or less (or £2,125 if let jointly), put 'X' in the box

Furnished holiday lettings (FHL) in the UK or European Economic Area (EEA)

Please read the **UK property notes** before filling in boxes 5 to 19. You need to fill in one page for UK businesses and a separate page for EEA businesses.

5 Income - *the amount of rent and any income for services provided to tenants*
£ · 0 0

6 Rent paid, repairs, insurance and costs of services provided - *the total amount*
£ · 0 0

7 Loan interest and other financial costs
£ · 0 0

8 Legal, management and other professional fees
£ · 0 0

9 Other allowable property expenses
£ · 0 0

10 Private use adjustment - *if expenses include any amounts for non-business purposes*
£ · 0 0

11 Balancing charges - *read the notes*
£ · 0 0

12 Capital allowances - *read the notes*
£ · 0 0

13 Adjusted profit for the year (if the amount in box 5 + box 10 + box 11 minus (boxes 6 to 9 + box 12) is positive)
£ · 0 0

14 Loss brought forward used against this year's profits - *if you have a non-FHL property business loss read the notes on property losses*
£ · 0 0

15 Taxable profit for the year (box 13 minus box 14)
£ · 0 0

16 Loss for the year (if the amount in boxes 6 to 9 + box 12 minus (box 5 + box 10 + box 11) is positive)
£ · 0 0

17 Total loss to carry forward
£ · 0 0

18 If this business is in the EEA, put 'X' in the box - *read the notes*

19 If you want to make a period of grace election, put 'X' in the box

Property income

Do not include furnished holiday lettings, Real Estate Investment Trust or Property Authorised Investment Funds dividends/distributions here.

20 Total rents and other income from property

£ [   ] · [0] [0]

21 Tax taken off any income in box 20 – *read the notes*

£ [   ] · [0] [0]

22 Premiums for the grant of a lease – from box E on the Working Sheet – *read the notes*

£ [   ] · [0] [0]

23 Reverse premiums and inducements

£ [   ] · [0] [0]

Property expenses

24 Rent, rates, insurance, ground rents etc.

£ [   ] · [0] [0]

25 Property repairs and maintenance

£ [   ] · [0] [0]

26 Loan interest and other financial costs

£ [   ] · [0] [0]

27 Legal, management and other professional fees

£ [   ] · [0] [0]

28 Costs of services provided, including wages

£ [   ] · [0] [0]

29 Other allowable property expenses

£ [   ] · [0] [0]

Calculating your taxable profit or loss

30 Private use adjustment – *read the notes*

£ [   ] · [0] [0]

31 Balancing charges – *read the notes*

£ [   ] · [0] [0]

32 Annual Investment Allowance

£ [   ] · [0] [0]

33 Business Premises Renovation Allowance (Assisted Areas only) – *read the notes*

£ [   ] · [0] [0]

34 All other capital allowances

£ [   ] · [0] [0]

35 Landlord's Energy Saving Allowance

£ [   ] · [0] [0]

36 10% wear and tear allowance – *for furnished residential accommodation only*

£ [   ] · [0] [0]

37 Rent a Room exempt amount

£ [   ] · [0] [0]

38 Adjusted profit for the year – from box O on the Working Sheet – *read the notes*

£ [   ] · [0] [0]

39 Loss brought forward used against this year's profits

£ [   ] · [0] [0]

40 Taxable profit for the year (box 38 minus box 39)

£ [   ] · [0] [0]

41 Adjusted loss for the year – from box O on the Working Sheet – *read the notes*

£ [   ] · [0] [0]

42 Loss set off against 2013–14 total income – *this will be unusual – read the notes*

£ [   ] · [0] [0]

43 Loss to carry forward to following year, including unused losses brought forward

£ [   ] · [0] [0]

 **HM Revenue & Customs**

Capital gains summary
Tax year 6 April 2013 to 5 April 2014

1	Your name

2	Your Unique Taxpayer Reference (UTR)

Summary of your enclosed computations

Please read the *Capital gains summary notes* before filling in this section. **You must enclose your computations, including details of each gain or loss, as well as filling in the boxes.**

ℹ To get notes and helpsheets that will help you fill in this form, go to hmrc.gov.uk/selfassessmentforms

3 Total gains *(Boxes 21 + 27 + 33 + 34)*
£ . 0 0

4 Gains qualifying for Entrepreneurs' Relief (but excluding gains deferred from before 23 June 2010) – *read the notes*
£ . 0 0

5 Gains invested under Seed Enterprise Investment Scheme and qualifying for exemption – *read the notes*
£ . 0 0

6 Total losses of the year – *enter '0' if there are none*
£ . 0 0

7 Losses brought forward and used in the year
£ . 0 0

8 Adjustment to Capital Gains Tax – *read the notes*
£ . 0 0

9 Additional liability for non-resident or dual resident trusts
£ . 0 0

10 Losses available to be carried forward to later years
£ . 0 0

11 Losses used against an earlier year's gain (special circumstances apply – *read the notes*)
£ . 0 0

12 Losses used against income – amount claimed against 2013-14 income – *read the notes*
£ . 0 0

13 Amount in box 12 relating to shares to which Enterprise Investment Scheme/Seed Enterprise Investment Scheme relief is attributable
£ . 0 0

14 Losses used against income – amount claimed against 2012-13 income – *read the notes*
£ . 0 0

15 Amount in box 14 relating to shares to which Enterprise Investment Scheme/Seed Enterprise Investment Scheme relief is attributable
£ . 0 0

16 Income losses of 2013-14 set against gains
£ . 0 0

17 Deferred gains from before 23 June 2010 qualifying for Entrepreneurs' Relief
£ . 0 0

Listed shares and securities

18 Number of disposals - *read the notes*

19 Disposal proceeds

£   · 0 0

20 Allowable costs (including purchase price)

£   · 0 0

21 Gains in the year, before losses

£   · 0 0

22 If you are making any claim or election, put 'X' in the box

23 If your computations include any estimates or valuations, put 'X' in the box

Unlisted shares and securities

24 Number of disposals - *read the notes*

25 Disposal proceeds

£   · 0 0

26 Allowable costs (including purchase price)

£   · 0 0

27 Gains in the year, before losses

£   · 0 0

28 If you are making any claim or election, put 'X' in the box

29 If your computations include any estimates or valuations, put 'X' in the box

Property and other assets and gains

30 Number of disposals

31 Disposal proceeds

£   · 0 0

32 Allowable costs (including purchase price)

£   · 0 0

33 Gains in the year, before losses

£   · 0 0

34 Attributed gains where personal losses cannot be set off

£   · 0 0

35 If you are making any claim or election, put 'X' in the box

36 If your computations include any estimates or valuations, put 'X' in the box

Any other information

37 Please give any other information in this space

Index

for your notes